ENGLISH IN LOS ANGELES

WRITTEN BY
PIERA FUMAGALLI

Copyright © 2011 by Piera Fumagalli

Printed by CreateSpace, Charleston, SC, 2013.

Trade Paperback   ISBN-13: 978-1483953281
ISBN-10: 1483953289

All rights reserved. No part of this publication, except the images noted in the picture credits (CC, GNU, PD, and MS), may be reproduced or transmitted in any form or by any means without permission in writing from Piera Fumagalli.

info@englishinlosangeles.com

Cover design by Barbara Fumagalli

FOR LINKS TO SUPPLEMENTARY VIDEOS, LISTENING COMPREHENSION QUIZZES, AND INTERACTIVE EXERCISES, VISIT THE COMPANION WEBSITE:

EnglishinLosAngeles.com

What every tourist and immigrant in this city has in common is Los Angeles itself. This textbook aims to engage English language learners in meaningful communication through exploration and contemplation of what made this vibrant city what it is today. In my more than thirty years of teaching English learners both here and abroad, I have understood that adults need clear explanations of sentence structure and dynamic activities to stimulate conversation. In addition, they need to be confronted with ideas that will trigger critical thinking. The companion website, EnglishinLosAngeles.com, provides interactive exercises and links to videos for listening comprehension and discussion. This textbook can be used in a classroom setting or independently as a guide to the language and sights of Los Angeles.

Piera Fumagalli

TABLE OF CONTENTS
CONVERSATION

Elephants never forget. KEEP AN EYE ON ME FOR THINGS TO REMEMBER

Welcome to Los Angeles	1
1. Meet Your Classmates	3
2. Let's Talk about Cities	4
Comparatives	5
Equatives	10
Articles	11
"To Be"	14
Superlatives	15
A List of Adjectives	17
Let's Use Adjectives	18
A Little, a Few, Much, and Many, So, Such, and Too	19
A Review of Verbs	21
Present and Past Tenses	21
Modal Auxiliaries (Helping Verbs)	22
Future: Will and Going to	23
3. Let's Talk about People	24
The Present Perfect	26
Single-word Adverbs of Frequency	27
A List of Irregular Past Tense Verbs	29
For and Since	32
Adverbs	35
4. Let's Talk about the Bravest Celebrity	39
Past Continuous	40
Focus on Questions	44
5. Let's Give Advice	49
Should	49
6. Let's Talk about the Lottery	56
If : The Real Conditional	56
7. Let's Talk about Obligations, Rules and Regulations	62
Must, Have to, and Have Got to	62
Must Not and Don't Have to	66
8. Let's Talk about Our Activities	70
Get, Do, Take and Make	70
9. Let's Talk about Experiences and Emotions	72
Adjectives Ending in "ed" and "ing"	73
10. Let's Talk without Mentioning Names	74
The Passive Voice	74
Review	77

i

EXPLORATION

11. Getting around Town	78
On Foot	78
By Bus	83
12. Prehistoric California: La Brea Tar Pits	84
Speaking about Habits in the Past: Used to + Verb	88
Expressions with Go + Verb+ing	89
13. The First People	90
The Gabrielinos, Tataviam, and Chumash	90
What Do You Have to Have?	96
The Iroquois League and the U.S. Federal System	97
14. El Camino Real	100
It Takes Time	101
15. El Pueblo de Los Angeles and Olvera Street	102
Asking for Prices	107
16. The San Fernando Mission	108
17. Leonis Adobe	111
18. Andres and Romulo Pico Adobe	115
The Orcutt Ranch	116
Review Vocabulary Puzzle #1	118
19. The Gene Autry National Center	120
20. The Los Angeles Zoo and Botanical Gardens	123
21. The Griffith Observatory	128
22. The Getty Museums	130
The J. Paul Getty Center	130
The Getty Villa near Malibu	133
23. The Beaches	135
Go, to Go, and Going to the Beach	136
24. Blue Jeans	139
25. The Nethercutt Museum: Cars, Cars, and More Cars	141
26. The Farmers Market	143
27. Exploring the Streets of LA	146
Prepositions	149
28. Fast Food: McDonald's and Burger King	151
29. Chili's Bar and Grill	154
30. Starbucks	157
31. A Change in Diet	160
Review Vocabulary Puzzle #2	161
Vocabulary Index	163
Key	168
Picture Credits	174
Bibliography	179

LEARNING OBJECTIVES
CONVERSATION

CHAPTERS	SPEAKING	GRAMMAR	VOCABULARY	READING	WRITING	CRITICAL THINKING
Welcome 1-2 (pages 1-23)	Asking for information Describing Making comparisons Expressing opinions Expressing extremes	**Review:** The verb "to be" Verbs, past and present Modal auxiliaries: will, would, can, could, may, might Questions WH-questions **Comparisons Equatives Superlatives Articles**	Adjectives to describe people, places, and things	An overview of tourist attractions in Los Angeles	Compare LA to another city First impressions	
3 (pages 24-38)	Discussing experiences Discussing competencies and abilities	**Present perfect Single-word adverbs of frequency Irregular past tense For/since Adverbs**	Adverbs of frequency and adverbs of manner	A comparison of singers		Discipline, goals, self-esteem, and charity
4 (pages 39-48)	Discussing activities in progress Keeping a conversation going Interrogation	**Past continuous Questions**	Action verbs	Lessons to learn from a celebrity	Write about a person you admire Describe actions in a picture	Bravery and unpopular causes Lessons from our elders Drawing conclusions
5 (pages 49-55)	Giving advice	**Should Review:** The present perfect For/since	Recommendations			Solving problems
6 (pages 56-61)	Discussing real possibilities Discussing superstitions	**The real conditional**	Optimism and pessimism		Pair work: write a story	Charitable causes Solving a problem
7 (pages 62-69)	Discussing rules and regulations	**Must/must not Have to/don't have to Have got to Had to Review:** Should	Legal and illegal activities	Employees' skills and experience		Who deserves a promotion? Whom should we lay off?
8 (pages 70-71)	Discussing activities	**Get, Do, Take, and Make**	Everyday activities			Planning for survival
9 (pages 72-73)	Discussing fears, phobias, and emotions	**-ED and -ING adjectives**	Everyday experiences and feelings	Phobias		
10 (pages 74-77)	Speaking without mentioning names	**Passive voice Review:** If + will Adverbs Should Present perfect Passive voice	Grown, raised, made, manufactured, invented	Children making mistakes		

iii

EXPLORATION

CHAPTERS	SPEAKING	GRAMMAR	VOCABULARY	READING	WRITING	CRITICAL THINKING
11 (pages 78-83)	Giving and understanding maps, directions, and how to take the bus	**Questions and answers**	Shops and businesses in the neighborhood	Long dialogues: getting around on foot and getting around by bus	**Please see below for writing suggestions**	
12 (pages 84-89)	Habits in the past	**used to+verb go+verb+ing**	Animals and prehistoric animals; the La Brea Tar Pits	Ice Age fossils and prehistoric Los Angeles		
13 (pages 90-99)	Expressing necessity	**have to+verb**	Native Americans: life, philosophy, and laws	The First People in Los Angeles; The Iroquois League		Life principles Laws, women's right to vote, peace
14 (pages 100-101)	Expressing time required	**It takes (time)**		El Camino Real		
15 (pages 102-107)	Asking for prices	**Singular/plural: How much does/do it/they cost?**	Early Los Angeles	El Pueblo de Los Angeles		Problems between ethnic groups Careful buying
16 (pages 108-110)			Farming, early mission life	The San Fernando Mission		
17 (pages 111-114)	Discussion, debate and/or role play		Early settlers, inheritance, and land claims	Leonis Adobe		Killing and cheating for money Inheritance Ghosts
18 (pages 115-119)	Discussion		A geological discovery Vocabulary review puzzle	Pico Adobe and the Orcutt Ranch		Time in nature The population explosion
19 (pages 120-122)	Discussion and decision-making		Cowboys and the West	Gene Autry		Moral values Work ethic
20 (pages 123-127)	Discussion, cooperation and compromise	**Review:** if + will comparatives should+ verb must+ verb have to + verb don't have to + verb	Animals and protection of them	The zoo and endangered condors		Endangered species Management and cooperation
21 (pages 128-129)	Discussion of social obligations		Land settlement and duties	Griffith Observatory		Use of land Debts to society Preserving the earth/helping society
22 (pages 130-134)	Agreeing and disagreeing		Media in art	The Getty Museums		The importance of beauty
23 (pages 135-138)	Expressing preferences and plans	Verb patterns with two verbs: **verb+ verb verb+ to + verb verb+ verb+ ing**	Tourism and the ocean	The beaches		

CHAPTERS	SPEAKING	GRAMMAR	VOCABULARY	READING	WRITING	CRITICAL THINKING
24 (pages 139-140)	Discussion of fashion		Fashion	The history of blue jeans		Fashion and traditional clothing
25 (pages 141-142)	Discussion of beauty		Cars	The Nethercutt Museum		What we leave behind at the end of life / The size of an ideal city
26 (pages 143-145)			Fruits and vegetables	The Farmers Market		
27 (pages 146-150)	Expressing tastes in architecture and street art	**Prepositions**	Public art, murals, and graffiti	Exploring the streets	**Please see below for writing suggestions**	Accidents and creativity / Public and artistic expression
28 (pages 151-153)	Giving advice on diets		Foods, plastics, and recycling	McDonald's and Burger King		Diets / Recycling
29 (pages 154-156)	Ordering in a restaurant		Restaurants	Chili's		Food allergies/ intolerances / Invention
30 (pages 157-159)	Discussion of marketing		Ingredients, light bulbs, and conscientious business	Starbucks		Missions in life / Carbon footprints / Business plans
31 (pages 160-162)	Discussion of changes in diet			A change in diet		Food customs and intolerances

Note: Although "Conversation" should be studied in sequence, chapters from "Exploration" can be taught in any order, depending on the interests of the class.

Listening skills are in the online component, *EnglishinLosAngeles.com*.

Writing skills may be addressed further by having the students write responses to critical thinking topics, or having them write their impressions of trips or videos.

Collage writing may be a way to introduce students to essay writing. One of the main problems in essays from beginning writers is the lack of concrete support for vicious circles of boring generalities. After a field trip or a virtual trip (viewing of a video), students can be encouraged to write a paragraph about one small part of the trip. They should answer as many of the six major questions as possible (Who, what, when, where, why, and how?) as well as write detailed descriptions (What does it look/sound/feel/ smell/taste like?). They can be encouraged to use metaphors, similes, and analogies.

Small detailed paragraphs from individual students may be pieced together like a collage to give a complete impression from the class. The teacher can collect the paragraphs and either divide them into sets of three compatible paragraphs, or have the class read them all and divide them into sets of three compatible paragraphs. As a class, the students can create an introduction and conclusion for the three paragraphs to construct a five-paragraph essay. Later, after practice, students can be divided into groups to create together the introductions and conclusions for sets of paragraphs. After practice, the students will be able to write five-paragraph essays by themselves.

WELCOME TO LOS ANGELES!

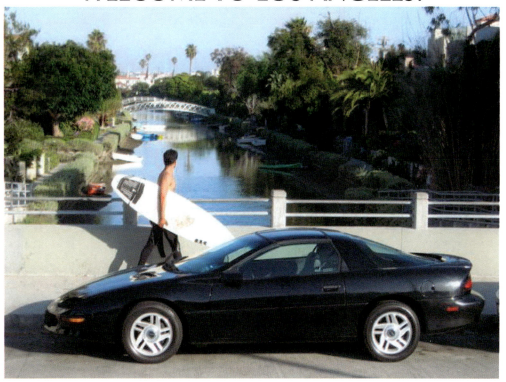

MANY CITIES FORM GREATER LOS ANGELES: HERE IS A CANAL IN VENICE, CALIFORNIA

If you think that Los Angeles is all about the glitz and glamour of Hollywood, you are in for a surprise. Of course, you can look for the stars on the Hollywood Walk of Fame and you can visit Universal Studios, where many movies are produced. You can even go indoor skydiving at Universal Studios City Walk, but there is another even wilder side of Los Angeles. You can see wild animals such as deer, hawks, coyotes, and rattlesnakes in Griffith Park, the largest natural area inside a city in the United States.

A VIEW OF DOWNTOWN LOS ANGELES FROM GRIFFITH PARK

Nature lovers can take it easy at Descanso Gardens, 160 acres of flowers and trees. One weekend in July, you can pick oranges and grapefruit at the Orcutt Ranch. You can also surf at the beach, and in winter, you can drive a few miles to ski in the mountains.

In Exposition Park, you can relax in the Rose Garden, visit the African American Museum, and go to the California Science Center to see the space shuttle Endeavor. Study California history, dinosaurs, mammals, birds, and insects at the Natural History Museum, or see a film in the 7-story IMAX Theater.

Learn about prehistoric Ice Age plants and animals at the Rancho La Brea Tar Pits. Explore history by touring the Chumash Museum, Olvera Street, the San Fernando Mission, and Leonis Adobe. Art lovers can visit MOCA (Museum of Contemporary Art), LACMA (LA County Museum of Art), the Getty Center, or time-travel to ancient Rome by visiting the Getty Villa, which is a reconstruction of a 2,000-year-old private house originally built in Herculaneum, Italy.

DESCANSO GARDENS

Car lovers have to visit the Petersen Automotive Museum or the Nethercutt Museum. Ship lovers can visit the Los Angeles Maritime Museum in San Pedro, or can go to Long Beach to tour the Queen Mary, an old passenger ship from 1936.

You already know about Disneyland, but don't forget Six Flags Magic Mountain, where you will find the tallest and fastest roller coasters in the world.

CONVERSATION

1. Meet Your Classmates

Try to find a friend who does not speak your language. If you go out to tour Los Angeles with your family, invite this friend. Everyone will have to speak English. Studying English will be painless!

ASK A QUESTION
QUESTION WORD + "IS, ARE, WAS, WERE" + SUBJECT

What is (he/she/it) _____ ?
What are (you/we/they) _____ ?

PUT THE FOLLOWING WORDS IN THE CORRECT ORDER TO FORM A QUESTION:

1. NAME / IS / WHAT / YOUR ?

   What is your name?

2. CITY / YOU / FROM / WHAT / ARE ?

   _____

3. YOUR / NUMBER / TELEPHONE / IS / WHAT?

   _____

4. ADDRESS / SKYPE / IS / YOUR / WHAT?

   _____

5. EMAIL / YOUR / IS / WHAT / ADDRESS?

   _____

6. CITY / WHAT / IS / FAVORITE / YOUR?

   _____

7. LIKE / WHAT / YOUR / IS / FAVORITE / CITY?

   _____

ASK YOUR CLASSMATES THE ABOVE QUESTIONS AND FILL IN THE CHART.
Don't force anyone to give out telephone numbers or addresses!
If you don't want to give out telephone numbers or addresses, just say, "I'd rather not say."
ASK YOUR FRIEND TO DESCRIBE HIS/HER FAVORITE CITY IN A FEW WORDS.

NAME	CITY (HOMETOWN)	TELEPHONE NUMBER	SKYPE ADDRESS	EMAIL ADDRESS	FAVORITE CITY	DESCRIPTION OF THE CITY

2. Let's Talk about Cities

FOCUS ON SENTENCE STRUCTURE:

- **Maria:** What is Daejong like?
- **Eun Ae:** It is an important city for research and technology. What is Mexico City like?
- **Maria:** It is very beautiful.

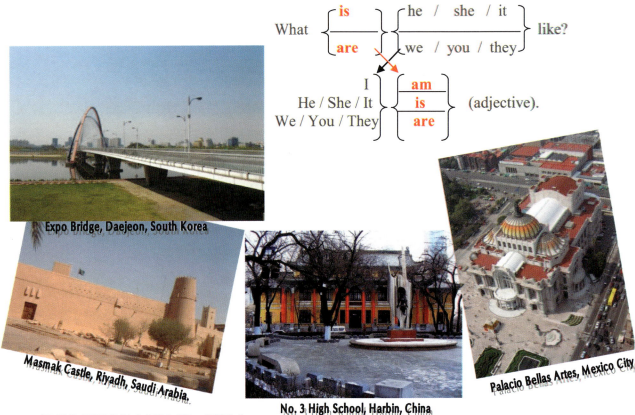

Expo Bridge, Daejeon, South Korea

Masmak Castle, Riyadh, Saudi Arabia

No. 3 High School, Harbin, China

Palacio Bellas Artes, Mexico City

DESCRIBE YOUR CITY

- **Maria:** What is (your hometown) like?
- **Chen:** It's big, busy, noisy, beautiful, exciting, and cosmopolitan.
- **Maria:** How big is it?
- **Chen:** The population of my city is four million.

big	new	busy	beautiful
calm	nice	chilly	cosmopolitan
cheap	old	cloudy	dangerous
clean	poor	dirty	exciting
cold	rich	noisy	expensive
cool	safe	pretty	interesting
dry	small	rainy	modern
hot	warm	sunny	polluted
large	wet	windy	romantic

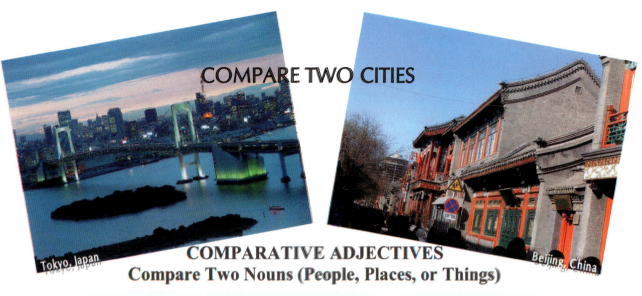

COMPARE TWO CITIES

COMPARATIVE ADJECTIVES
Compare Two Nouns (People, Places, or Things)

- **Cheng:** Beijing is bigger than Tokyo.
- **Koko:** Yes, but Tokyo is more interesting than Beijing.
- **Cheng:** I don't think so. Beijing is more interesting than Tokyo.

| ___tall___ -er than

 ___pretti___ -er than

 Use "–er" with one-syllable adjectives:
 New York is colder than Los Angeles.
 Use "–er" with two-syllable adjectives that end in "y"
 (change the "y" to "i" and add "er"):
 Chicago is windier than Los Angeles. | more ___beautiful___ than

 Use "more" with two- (or more) syllable adjectives that do NOT end in "y":

 Chicago is more cosmopolitan than Dallas.
 New Orleans is more exciting than Fresno.
 Los Angeles is more interesting than Fargo.
 New York is more expensive than Omaha. |

Exceptions that follow a rule:

For adjectives that end in "**le**":	For adjectives that end in "**ow**":
simp**le** → simp**le**r	narr**ow** → narr**ow**er
litt**le** → litt**le**r	yell**ow** → yell**ow**er

Crazy Exceptions:

bad	worse
good	better
far	farther

FOCUS ON SPELLING:

For a word ending in a stressed syllable with one vowel (a/e/i/o/u) followed by one consonant, **DOUBLE THE CONSONANT**: one vowel (Exceptions: w, x, y. Ex. =slower)
one consonant
BIG = BI**GG**ER

1 vowel + 1 consonant	1 vowel + 2 consonants	2 vowels + 1 consonant
fat → fa**tt**er (double)	short → shorter	clean → cleaner
thin → thi**nn**er (double)	warm → warmer	neat → neater

Los Angeles is { _____er / more _____ } than . . . .

Photo by Joseph Plotz

HANCOCK PARK STREET

Adjective + -ER	MORE + Adjective
city: pretty / ugly / fancy	city: historic / modern / dangerous
weather: chilly / windy / hot / cold / warm	people: energetic / relaxed / nervous
streets: wide / narrow / clean / dirty	reserved / outgoing
noisy / quiet / busy / calm / safe	environment: beautiful / natural / romantic
buildings: old / new / tall	boring / exciting / interesting
air: smoggy / clean / fresh	polluted / crowded / spacious

Write down a few of your ideas to share with your partner and then with the class:

_____

_____

_____

_____

Count the syllables: one, or ending in "y" **-ER** / two + **MORE.**

COMPARE TWO PLACES OR THINGS

- **Cheng:** Jeans are more comfortable than a dress.
- **Koko:** Yes, but a dress is prettier than jeans.

Look at the pictures. Work with a partner. Discuss which one you like better and why. You may use the vocabulary below.

(add –er)	(add –er)	(add more . . .)	(add more . . .)
cheap	quiet	beautiful	exciting
cute	safe	comfortable	expensive
fast	slow	convenient	powerful
friendly	strong	dangerous	relaxing
pretty	tasty	delicious	reliable
noisy	weak	efficient	useful

1.

   A LAND LINE   A CELL PHONE OR MOBILE PHONE

2.

   A CRUISE OR A VACATION ON A CRUISE SHIP   A VACATION BY TRAIN

3.

   A SMALL DOG (A CHIHUAHUA)   A BIG DOG (A GERMAN SHEPHERD)

4.

   A PICNIC   A MEAL IN A RESTAURANT

INTERVIEW TWO CLASSMATES

This is a speaking exercise. Interview two of your classmates and write their opinions in the box. Just write a word or two—not a whole sentence. Spend your time speaking.

- **Abdulaziz:** Which is more important: love or money?
- **Tingting:** Love is more important than money.

QUESTION	NAME	NAME
Which is more difficult: reading English or listening to English?		
Which is more frightening: a spider or a snake?		
Which is more lovable: a cat or a dog?		
Who is usually more popular: a fashionable person or a friendly person?		
Which is more important: breakfast or lunch?		
Which is more exciting: a trip to Disneyland or a trip to a museum?		
Which is more important: helping a friend or studying for an exam?		
Which is more romantic: a date at a restaurant or a date at a nightclub?		
Which is easier: emailing or texting?		
Which is more useful: a laptop or a smart phone?		
Which is more important: love or money?		
Which is better: a car or a bicycle?		
Which is nicer: a birthday card or a birthday phone call?		
Which is more important: a printer or an iPad?		
Which are more efficient: chopsticks or a fork and knife?		
Which is more satisfying: a cola or a cup of coffee?		

SURVEY: ASK QUESTIONS USING COMPARATIVE ADJECTIVES

Question:
In your opinion, is/are _____ { _____-er than / more _____ than } _____ ?

Answer:
In my opinion, _____ is/are { _____-er than / more _____ than } _____ .

- **Mohammed:** In your opinion, is classical music more beautiful than rock music?
- **Mario:** In my opinion, rock music is more beautiful than classical music.

Keep track of your survey results.
Make a mark for the opinion of each person you interview:

| Ex. | classical music
IIII | rock music
NN I | beautiful |

#			
1.	a good income	an interesting job	important
2.	a happy family life	a good job	important
3.	close friends	a lot of money	important
4.	a safe neighborhood	a beautiful apartment	important
5.	an orange	a cookie	delicious
6.	a salad	French fries	tasty
7.	a good movie	a good book	interesting
8.	a diamond ring	a rose	beautiful
9.	Chinese food	American food	delicious
10.	good schools	beautiful parks	important
11.	an afternoon in a garden	an afternoon in a mall	interesting
12.	tennis	volleyball	easy
13.	math (mathematics)	history	difficult
14.	jazz	classical music	beautiful
15.	red	pink	pretty
16.	basketball	soccer	exciting
17.	clothes	food	important

EQUATIVES: WHEN TWO THINGS ARE SIMILAR

Bob and Bill are the same height.　　**Tom and Jack are NOT the same height.**

Bob is **as** <u>tall</u> **as** Bill.

Using only "as _____ as," how can you compare Tom and Jack?

_____ as _____ as _____

- **Abdulaziz:** Do you think New York City is more interesting than New Orleans?
- **Tingting:** They are very different, but New Orleans is **as interesting as** New York City.

Manhattan, New York City

Bourbon Street, New Orleans

Photo by Jon Sullivan

Never use "-er," "more," or "than" between "as _ as."

FOCUS ON ARTICLES
a   an   the

	INDEFINITE (with count nouns only)	DEFINITE (with count & non-count nouns)
SINGULAR	<u>a</u> book - <u>an</u> apple (for vowel sounds)	<u>the</u> book
PLURAL	books	<u>the</u> books

> **1. Singular count nouns are rarely used without an article, "this" or "that," or a possessive adjective.**
>
> **<u>If it is a singular count noun, it needs something in front!</u>**
>
> **A** dog is a good friend. **That** dog was black. **My** dog is white.

DETAILS:

2. **Do not use "a" or "an" with plural count nouns. "A" and "an" mean "one."**
   I like dogs. (This means I like all dogs, not any particular dog.)

3. **A singular non-count noun without an article means "all" or "any" (not special or particular).**
   Gold is expensive. (This means all gold is expensive.)

4. **Do not use articles with possessives.**
   Did you see John's car? It's fancy, but my car is as reliable as his.

Articles give meaning. "Dog is good" means that in this sentence, "dog" is not a count noun. This means: "Dog <u>meat</u> is good."

5. **Use the indefinite article if the speaker or the listener does not know** *which*.
   I saw a dog yesterday. (The listener does not know *which* dog.)
   The perfume you are wearing smells good. (The listener knows which perfume.)

6. **The first time the speaker talks about something, he/she uses the indefinite article. Later, when the listener knows** *which,* **the speaker uses the definite article. Use "the" when details are given.**
   I bought a book yesterday. The book is about growing roses. The coffee Jane drinks is good.

7. **We use "the" for places in our neighborhood or things in our everyday life even though the listener does not know exactly** *which*. **The listener understands "my usual."**
   I have to go to the post office today, and I have to take the bus to the doctor.

8. **We don't need to use an article when we talk about the usual work, school, church, bed, or the usual breakfast, lunch, dinner or supper.**
   I go to school in Los Angeles. When are you going to have dinner?

9. **Don't use an article with** *proper nouns*. **If these names are used as** *adjectives*, **use an article.**
   Los Angeles is near the Pacific Ocean. But: The Los Angeles riots occurred in 1992.

10. **When names of mountain ranges, oceans/seas, and rivers include an adjective, use "the." Don't use "the" with continents such as North America. When countries include adjectives such as "united," "union," or "republic," use "the." (Also: use "the" for the Netherlands, the Philippines.)**
    If you drive across the United States, you will see the Mississippi River and the Rocky Mountains.

AN EXERCISE ON ARTICLES

Singular count nouns usually need articles. Put a check by all the count nouns.

☐ book   ☐ Coca-Cola   ☐ rice
☐ cheese   ☐ onion   ☐ sugar
☐ milk   ☐ bread   ☐ orange
☐ pencil   ☐ tomato   ☐ orange juice

Fill in the blanks with "a," "an," "the," or "-----" for no article.

1) _____ sugar is sweet. (See point # 3.)
2) _____ sugar I bought yesterday was expensive. (See point #6.)
3) _____ hamburgers can be bad for your health. (See point #2.)
4) I bought _____ jacket yesterday. _____ jacket is wool and very warm. (#1, #6)
5) _____ jackets are always useful in cold climates. (See point #2.)
6) _____ moon was beautiful last night. (We know which moon: our moon!)
7) _____ orange juice is good for you. (See point #3.)
8) _____ orange juice I squeezed this morning is delicious. (See point #6.)
9) _____ sun is hot in Los Angeles. (We know which sun: our sun!)
10) _____ water is necessary for life. (See point #3.)
11) Don't drink _____ water in that lake. (See point #6.)
12) Some people think a trip through _____ Europe is not complete without a few days in _____ Paris and _____ Rome. (See points #9 & #10.)
13) José is from _____ Dominican Republic. Ana is from _____ El Salvador. Hiromi is from _____ Japan. (See point #10.)
14) I have to go to _____ doctor after _____ work. I am going to take _____ bus to _____ school this evening. (See points #7 and #8.)
15) I live on _____ Fairfax Avenue. I take _____ Fairfax bus every day. I shop at _____ Fairfax stores every day after _____ work. (See points #8 and #9.)
16) Robert is going to buy _____ dog this year. (See point #5.)
17) I met _____ woman in _____ post office. _____ woman works in _____ library in my neighborhood. She is going to help me find _____ good book in English for _____ my children. (See points #4, #5, #6, #7.)
18) _____ Los Angeles gets some water from _____ Colorado River. (#9 & #10)
19) _____ red wine is good for your heart. _____ red wine you bought is tasty. (#3 & #6)
20) I have to go to _____ supermarket. I need to buy _____ wine, _____ sugar, _____ oranges, _____ raisins and _____ butter. (See #3 & #7.)
21) I rarely drink _____ coffee, but _____ coffee Jane makes is delicious. (See point #3 & #6.)
22) I read _____ (same) newspaper every day. (See #7.)
23) If you want to be _____ secretary, you have to know how to use computer software. (See point #5.)
24) She is _____ best secretary I know. (See point #6.)
25) She is looking for _____ apartment with _____ balcony. (See point #5.)

A singular count noun needs an article, a possessive pronoun, or this/that!

REVIEW (fill in the blanks with an article, no article, or a form of the adjective)

1. Los Angeles is _____ (hot) than Paris.
2. Paris is _____ (romantic) than Chicago.
3. _____ good student watches videos and movies outside of class.
4. _____ silver is _____ (cheap) than _____ gold.
5. I went to _____ supermarket yesterday and I bought _____ potatoes.
6. Los Angeles is _____ (busy) than Fresno.
7. Los Angeles is as _____ (exciting) as New York City.
8. Bakersfield is not as _____ (cosmopolitan) as Los Angeles.
9. _____ dog is _____ good friend.
10. My brother isn't as _____ (polite) as my sister.
11. Seoul is _____ (big) than San Diego.
12. Descanso Gardens is _____ (relaxing) than a mall.
13. _____ ice cream is as _____ (delicious) as cake.
14. Some people eat _____ bread and others eat _____ rice.
15. If you drive across _____ United States, you should stop to see _____ Grand Canyon and _____ Rocky Mountains.
16. _____ sugar is _____ (sweet) than coffee.
17. _____ dog is _____ (friendly) than _____ cat.
18. I never drink _____ coffee after dinner because it keeps me awake.
19. _____ texting is _____ (convenient) than emailing.
20. _____ book is _____ (interesting) than _____ movie.
21. _____ love is _____ (important) than _____ money.
22. Some people think _____ biology is _____ (difficult) than _____ history.
23. _____ French fries are _____ (tasty) than _____ cookies.
24. _____ Nevada is _____ state near _____ California.
25. _____ Coca-Cola is _____ (bad) for your health than _____ juice.

> Remember: Use –er with one-syllable adjectives & those ending in "y"; use "more" with two-syllable adjectives.

FOCUS ON THE VERB "TO BE"

- **Michael:** Have you visited Disneyland? It **is** "the happiest place on earth."
- **Chen:** No, I haven't. **Is** Disneyland in Los Angeles?
- **Michael:** No, it **is** about 25 miles from Los Angeles, in Anaheim.
- **Chen:** Why **is** it so far away?
- **Michael:** It **was** <u>built</u> outside the city because Walt Disney needed a large area of land to build his dream amusement park.
- **Chen:** Who **is** Walt Disney and what **is** he do**ing** now?
- **Michael:** Walt Disney died in 1966. He **was** an artist, an animator, and a movie producer. Along with his brother Roy, he created the Walt Disney Company.

Remember to conjugate the verb correctly:

THE VERB "TO BE" - PRESENT	SINGULAR	PLURAL
FIRST PERSON	I am	we are
SECOND PERSON	you are	you are
THIRD PERSON	he is she is it is	they are

THE VERB "TO BE" - PAST	SINGULAR	PLURAL
FIRST PERSON	I was	we were
SECOND PERSON	you were	you were
THIRD PERSON	he was she was it was	they were

We use the verb "to be" in four main ways:

1. **with a noun** (person, place, or thing)

   He <u>is</u> **a painter**.

2. **with an adjective**

   These roses <u>are</u> **beautiful**.

3. **with a verb + ing** (continuous or progressive tenses on pages 40-43)

   She <u>is</u> **fishing** now.
   She <u>was</u> **fishing** at 6:00 yesterday.

4. **with the passive voice** (on pages 74-76):

   The pyramids in Egypt <u>were</u> **built** thousands of years ago.

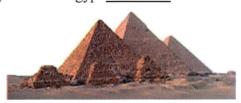

FOCUS ON SENTENCE STRUCTURE

REVIEW COMPARATIVE ADJECTIVES

Compare (TWO) Nouns (People, Places, or Things)

| **__tall__-er than**
 __pretti__-er than
 Use "–er" with one-syllable adjectives:

 The rose is darker than the daisy.
 New York is colder than Los Angeles.
 Use "–er" with two-syllable adjectives that end in "y"
 (change the "y" to "i" and add "er"):

 Chicago is windier than New York City.
 The rose is prettier than the daisy. | **more __beautiful__ than**

 Use "more" with two- (or more) syllable adjectives that do NOT end in "y":

 The rose is more beautiful than the daisy.
 Chicago is more cosmopolitan than Dallas.
 New Orleans is more exciting than Fresno.
 Los Angeles is more crowded than Fargo.
 New York is more expensive than Omaha.
 Las Vegas is noisier than Northridge. |

If you learn the above rules, the following will be easy!

LEARN SUPERLATIVE ADJECTIVES

Compare (THREE OR MORE) Nouns (People, Places, or Things)

| **the __tall__-est**
 the __pretti__-est
 Use "the ___ –est" with one-syllable adjectives:

 The rose is the tallest flower.

 Use "the ___ –est" with two-syllable adjectives that end in "y"
 (change the "y" to "i" and add "est"):

 The lily is the prettiest flower of the three. | **the most __beautiful__**

 Use "the most" with two- (or more) syllable adjectives that do NOT end in "y":

 The lily is the most beautiful flower of the three.
 The rose is the most dangerous flower because it has thorns.
 Sandra Bullock is the most generous actress I know. She gave a million dollars to the earthquake victims in Japan. |

Crazy Exceptions:	**(comparative)**	**(superlative)**
bad	worse	the worst
good	better	the best
far	farther	the farthest

SUPERLATIVES: A SPEAKING EXERCISE

This is a speaking exercise. **Speak** with your classmates and write his or her answers in the boxes. Then ask for an explanation. (Why? Can you tell me more? Why did you say that?) Just write a word or two—not a whole sentence. Spend your time speaking.

- **Mohammed:** Who is the most generous person you know?
- **Mario:** My sister is the most generous person I know. She always helps people in her family and in the community.

QUESTION	ANSWER	EXPLANATION
Who is the most generous person you know?		
Who is the most handsome actor?		
Who is the most beautiful actress?*		
Who is the most talented singer?		
Who is the richest person in your country?		
Who is the happiest person in your family?		
What is the most delicious fruit?		
What is the tastiest vegetable?		
What is the most interesting tourist attraction in your country?		
What is the tallest building in your city?		
What is the highest mountain in your country?		
What is the longest river in your country?		
What is the largest company in your country?		
What is the most popular video game?		
What is the most endangered animal in your country?		
What is the most important holiday in your country?		

*Traditionally, the word "actress" is for actors who are women/girls, although today some women and girls like to be called "actors."

HERE ARE SOME ADJECTIVES YOU CAN USE IN SPEAKING

The following adjectives are divided into groups for the most common usage.

ADJECTIVES TO DESCRIBE PEOPLE	MORE ADJECTIVES TO DESCRIBE PEOPLE	ADJECTIVES TO DESCRIBE PLACES	MORE ADJECTIVES TO DESCRIBE PLACES	ADJECTIVES TO DESCRIBE THINGS
attractive	light	attractive	old	attractive
bad	little	bad	popular	bad
beautiful	loud	beautiful	pretty	beautiful
big	magnificent	big	prosperous	big
bright	modern	bright	quiet	bright
busy	neat	busy	rich	cheap
capable	nice	cheap	romantic	clean
clean	noisy	clean	safe	comfortable
clumsy	old	comfortable	simple	convenient
comfortable	outgoing	convenient	small	cute
crazy	patient	cosmopolitan	tiny	dangerous
cute	polite	crazy	uncomfortable	efficient
dangerous	popular	cute	warm	elegant
dependable	powerful	dangerous	wealthy	enormous
difficult	pretty	efficient	wide	exciting
efficient	prosperous	elegant	wonderful	expensive
elegant	quiet	enormous		fancy
energetic	reliable	exciting		fantastic
enormous	rich	expensive		fashionable
exciting	romantic	fancy		fast
fancy	rude	fantastic		good
fantastic	short	fashionable		high
fashionable	sick	good		inexpensive
fast	simple	high		interesting
flexible	slow	hospitable		large
friendly	small	inexpensive		little
funny	smart	interesting		long
generous	stingy	large		magnificent
good	stupid	little		modern
graceful	sympathetic	long		neat
greedy	talented	loud		new
handsome	talkative	magnificent		nice
happy	tall	modern		old
healthy	tiny	neat		popular
heavy	uncomfortable	new		pretty
helpful	understanding	nice		safe
honest	useful	noisy		simple
hospitable	warm			slow
impolite	wealthy			small/tiny
intelligent	wonderful			uncomfortable
interesting	young			useful
kind				warm
large				wide
				wonderful

LET'S USE ADJECTIVES

Melrose Avenue, Los Angeles

- **Mary:** You said you like to shop. Did you go to Melrose Avenue?
- **Amy:** Are you **serious**? That's the first place I went. It's **so awesome**!
- **Mary:** And the fashions are **so cool**!
- **Amy:** Totally! They're **amazing**. But I didn't buy everything I wanted. I bought just **a few** scarves. Some of the shops are **too expensive**.
- **Mary:** I know: **so** many **cool** clothes and not **enough** money! But I always have **such** a **good** time when I go there.
- **Amy: True**. I had **so much** fun.

Some Americans use mainly three adjectives: "amazing," "awesome," and "cool." They all mean "great." The previous page has many adjectives you can use. Try to use many different adjectives.

Circle the correct adjective:
1. My friend Jack is very (prosperous / expensive).
2. I like your new sweater. It's (attractive / outgoing).
3. Mary is (tall / high).
4. I love that building. It is very (patient / modern).

THE WORDS "A LITTLE," "A FEW," "MUCH," AND "MANY"

Non-count nouns: How <u>much</u> sugar do you want? Just <u>a little</u>.
Count nouns: How <u>many</u> cherries do you want? Just <u>a few</u>.
Notice that plural count nouns end in "s"!

Exercise # 1: Circle the correct adjective:
1. When you go to the store, buy (a little / a few) cheese.
2. Can you recommend (a little / a few) good books?
3. I need to buy (a little / a few) bread.
4. I need to buy (a little / a few) loaves of bread.

WHAT'S THE DIFFERENCE BETWEEN "LITTLE" AND "A LITTLE" AND THE DIFFERENCE BETWEEN "FEW" AND "A FEW"?

"**Few**" and "**little**" express a negative idea of "**not many**" and "**not much**."
"**A few**" and "**a little**" simply mean "**some, a small number, or a small amount**."

Exercise # 2: Circle the correct adjective:
1. Los Angeles is great. There are (few / a few) reasons to travel to Las Vegas.
2. The food is not tasty. You need to add (little / a little) salt.
3. I like people. It's always nice to travel with (few / a few) good friends.
4. It's so easy! I'm going to need (little / a little) help.

THE COMPARATIVE ADJECTIVES "LESS" AND "FEWER"

Exercise # 3: Circle the correct adjective:
1. I need (less / fewer) books for this course.
2. Amy likes quieter restaurants with (less / fewer) noise.
3. I'm on a diet. I need to eat (less / fewer) cookies.
4. Jack spent (less / fewer) money this year than last year.*

THE WORDS "VERY," "SO," "SUCH," AND "TOO"

"**So**" has many meanings, but it often means "**very**" or "**what I see now.**"
   Don't drive **so** *fast*! Use "**so**" before *adjectives* and *adverbs*.
"**Such**" is like "**so**," but use "**such**" before <u>nouns</u> or before an adjective + <u>a noun</u>.
   It is **such** <u>a night</u>! There is **such** <u>a</u> beautiful <u>moon</u>!
"**Too**" means "**not right or bad for the time and place.**"
   When you are driving, 85 miles per hour is very fast.
   30 miles per hour is not very fast. 30 miles per hour is **too** slow
   for the freeway, but **too** fast near a school when there are children.

*We don't count money or time. We count dollars and cents. We count hours and minutes.

Exercise # 4: Circle the correct adjective:
1. She didn't help me because she was (very / too) busy.
2. Although she was (very / too) busy, she found time to help me.

FIRST IMPRESSIONS

By now you have been here just long enough to have some wonderful and strange first impressions of the United States. Write down a few of your first impressions. A month from now, you will feel different, so it is important to note what you are thinking today.

Date: _____

A REVIEW OF VERBS

MAIN VERBS:

- **Michael:** What did you do yesterday?
- **Chen:** <u>I walked</u> in Griffith Park and <u>visited</u> the Griffith Park Observatory.
- **Michael:** What are you doing now?
- **Chen:** I'm planning my sightseeing schedule for tomorrow. Do you have any suggestions?
- **Michael:** <u>You have</u> to see some movie stars in Hollywood.
- **Chen:** Are you serious? <u>I know</u> I can take a bus tour to see their homes, but I don't think it is possible to see movie stars unless you are very, very lucky.
- **Michael:** True, but you can see plenty of wax statues of movie stars in the Hollywood Wax Museum!

Remember to conjugate the verbs correctly:

"TO HAVE" - PRESENT		
	SINGULAR	PLURAL
FIRST PERSON	I have	we have
SECOND PERSON	you have	you have
THIRD PERSON	he has she has it has	they have

REGULAR VERBS - PRESENT		
	SINGULAR	PLURAL
FIRST PERSON	I work	we work
SECOND PERSON	you work	you work
THIRD PERSON	he works she works it works	they work

The past tense conjugation of regular verbs is simple. Just add "ed" for everyone! The pronunciation is not so simple. We have three ways to pronounce "ed":

REGULAR VERBS - PAST	
THE LAST SOUND OF THE VERB	PRONUNCIATION OF "ed"
is voiced (with vibrations)	d
is voiceless (without vibrations)	t
is "d" or "t"	ed

Put your hand on your throat and feel for vibrations.

WORD – PAST TENSE	THE END SOUND	PRONUNCIATION
listened	vibrations	listend
worked	no vibrations	workt
needed	d	needed
waited	t	waited

Exercise: how do you pronounce the following?
1. played 2. closed 3. dressed 4. ended 5. studied 6. lived 7. liked 8. hated

MODAL AUXILIARY (HELPING) VERBS

- **Chen:** I have one more day in Los Angeles. What <u>can</u> I <u>see</u> in one day?
- **Michael:** You <u>can</u> <u>see</u> the George C. Page Museum at the La Brea Tar Pits. You <u>will</u> never <u>see</u> so many Ice Age fossils anywhere else in the world.
- **Chen:** Ice Age fossils? I <u>might</u> <u>get</u> bored.
- **Michael:** I don't think you <u>will</u> <u>get</u> bored, but if you do, you <u>can</u> <u>visit</u> the Petersen Automotive Museum across the street.
- **Chen:** I'm not crazy about cars. <u>Could</u> you <u>help</u> me decide on some place else to go?
- **Michael:** If you don't like cars, you <u>might</u> <u>like</u> the art exhibits at the Los Angeles County Museum of Art. It's near the La Brea Tar Pits and the Petersen Automotive Museum.

Modal auxiliary (helping) verbs help another verb change its meaning. Let's take for an example the word "work." **I work (the simple present tense = every day/week, etc.).** Here are some meanings for the modal auxiliaries:

MODAL AUXILIARY	SENTENCE	MEANING
will	I will work. (I'll work.) NEGATIVE: I will not work. I won't work.	in the future
would	Would you work for me? I would work for good pay. (I'd work ....) I would work all night when I was younger. NEGATIVE: I would not work. I wouldn't work.	polite conditional conditional, future possibility past habit
can	I can work. NEGATIVE: I cannot work. I can't work.	know how, ability "Can" sometimes means "may."
could	Could you work for me? I could work if you pay me more. I could work hard when I was little. NEGATIVE: I could not work. I couldn't work.	polite conditional conditional, future possibility past of know how, ability
may	I may work when the doctor says I'm well.	permission "May" sometimes means "might."
might	I might work.	possibility

Never use "to" with modal auxiliaries. They are followed by a simple verb: no "s" and no "ing."

THE DIFFERENCE BETWEEN "WILL" AND "GOING TO"

WHEN YOU HAVE A PLAN USE: **GOING TO**	I'm going to visit Universal Studios tomorrow.
WHEN YOU HAVE NO PREVIOUS PLAN, OR WHEN YOU SUDDENLY VOLUNTEER TO DO SOMETHING, USE: **WILL**	• **Maria:** Where's the bus stop? • **Amy:** Don't worry. I'll help you find it.
WHEN YOU ARE MAKING A PREDICTION, USE: **GOING TO** OR **WILL**	It's going to rain tomorrow. It will rain tomorrow.

REVIEW (circle the correct answer)

1. LACMA is the (interesting/more interesting/most interesting) museum.
2. There are (so much/so many) tourist attractions in Los Angeles.
3. I am (so/very/too) tired to visit another tourist attraction.
4. Yesterday I (was visit/visited/visit) many tourist attractions.
5. Jack likes (a little/a few) sugar in his coffee.
6. He is (happy/enjoy) that he came to Los Angeles.
7. I planned my trip. Tomorrow I (will/going to/am going to) see the Getty.
8. Mary is (busy/busier/busiest) than Susan.
9. **Jack:** I can't read this map. **Tom:** I (will/going to/am going to) help you.
10. I want to spend (much/many) more time in museums and (less/fewer) time on the beach.
11. Jane thinks Venice is (so/such) a great beach, and Hollywood is (so/such) interesting.
12. I was (very/too) busy, but I had time to visit the Getty Villa.
13. I was (very/too) busy, and I didn't have time to visit the Getty Villa.
14. Bob (was go/went/go) to the La Brea Tar Pits yesterday.
15. Tom was (study/busy/studied) yesterday.
16. Who is the (talented/more talented/most talented) singer you know?
17. Is Taylor Swift as (talented/more talented/most talented) as Dolly Parton?
18. Who is (young/younger/more young/youngest/most young): Taylor Swift or Dolly Parton?
19. I would like to eat (fewer/less) fast food.
20. I would like to eat (fewer/less) potato chips.

3. Let's Talk about People

MICHAEL JACKSON
August 28, 1958 – June 25, 2009

One of the most talented performers ever, **Michael Jackson** was born in Gary, Indiana. When he was only five years old, he joined his brothers' band and soon became the lead singer and the star of the Jackson 5. With their father's guidance, the brothers polished their act and signed a contract with Motown records in 1968. Although he continued to work with his brothers, in 1971 Michael started his solo career. In 1972, his song about a rat, "Ben," became his first solo number one single.

Michael first danced his famous moonwalk during a performance of "Billie Jean" on a television special in 1982, and a year later, he forever changed the music industry with the release of his exciting video, "Thriller." All in all, he released 11 solo albums and won 13 Grammy Awards. He was married twice. The *Guinness Book of World Records* has many listings for Michael, including one for the best-selling album of all time, *Thriller*. In 1979, the Jacksons got a star on the Hollywood Walk of Fame. Michael got his own star in 1984, and you can see it at 6927 Hollywood Boulevard. If you look for his star, be careful! A radio personality with the same name has a star in a different place.

JANET JACKSON
May 16, 1966 –

Michael was eight years old when his youngest sister, **Janet Jackson**, was born in Gary, Indiana. She attended school in the San Fernando Valley (part of Los Angeles County), and first sang with her brothers on television in 1974. She released her first album in 1982. Since then, she **has recorded** numerous albums and **has won** many Grammy Awards. She **has** also **worked** as an actress, both in television and in movies.

Like her brother, she is very generous, and **has raised** money for charities. The lyrics of her songs speak about problems in the world such as injustice and illiteracy. She believes in discipline, and **has said**, "Discipline is a key to freedom. Discipline allows me—allows all of us—to focus."

She **has been married** twice. In spite of her talent, beauty, and success, her book, *True You,* reveals that she **has** always **had** problems with self-esteem. Her star is at 1500 Vine Street on the Hollywood Walk of Fame.

CRITICAL THINKING

1. When he was a child, Michael made friends with a rat. He sang, "They don't see you as I do; I wish they would try to." Why do you think he made friends with a rat?
2. How is discipline a key to freedom? Can you see how discipline can be a key to freedom in your life? (discipline=training to work hard to reach goals)
3. What are your goals in life? Is it difficult for you to focus on your goals?
4. Why do you think Janet has problems with self-esteem (a good feeling about herself)? Do these problems help or harm her? Do they make her work harder?
5. Would you like to raise money for any particular charities? Which? Why?

Focus on Sentence Structure: the Present Perfect

Subject + **have/has** + **past participle***
*the third form, the same as the past form for *regular* verbs

- **Abdulaziz:** I **have lived** in LA for six months. (HE LIVES IN LA NOW.)
- **Tingting:** I **lived** in LA for six years. (SHE DOESN'T LIVE IN LA NOW.)

THE PRESENT PERFECT
- is **never used** to describe dead people.
- is **never used** with dates of past events or words like "yesterday" or "ago."
- describes actions that start in the past and **continue into the present**, may continue into the future, or have just happened and are important in the present.
- describes actions that are part of what we consider the present time.

At a time when lunch is still possible (lunch can be in the middle of the day):

- **Abdulaziz:** **Have** you **eaten** lunch?
- **Tingting:** No, I **haven't**.
- **Abdulaziz:** Let's grab a bite before we go to the museum.

At a time when it is too late for lunch (if you eat, it will be dinner, not lunch):

- **Abdulaziz:** **Did** you **eat** lunch?
- **Tingting:** No, I **didn't**.
- **Abdulaziz:** You shouldn't skip lunch. It's bad for your health.

Review the paragraphs on the preceding pages about Michael and Janet Jackson. When was the present perfect used? Why was it never used when describing Michael?

A NOTE ON WORD ORDER FOR SINGLE-WORD ADVERBS OF FREQUENCY

The words "recently" and "just" often mean that the action is important in the present time; therefore, the present perfect tense is often used.

Single-word adverbs of frequency sometimes mean up to the present time, but not always. Think! Be careful!

"Ever" is used in questions, not usually in answers or statements unless with "not" or "hardly."

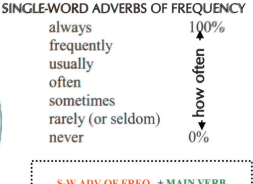

SINGLE-WORD ADVERBS OF FREQUENCY

always — 100%
frequently
usually
often
sometimes
rarely (or seldom)
never — 0%

← how often →

S-W ADV OF FREQ. + MAIN VERB

HELPING VERB + S-W ADV OF FREQ.

- **Ana:** Have you ever gone skateboarding?
- **Seung Hoon:** Yes, I have. I usually use a skateboard at the university. I can get to class much more quickly.
- **Ana:** Aren't you afraid? There have recently been some terrible skateboarding accidents.
- **Seung Hoon:** Don't be ridiculous. I have seldom seen an accident, and I am never afraid of using a skateboard.

Choose the past or the present perfect:
1. Recently there _____ (be) many tornadoes in the Midwest.
2. I _____ just _____ (order) a pizza. It will be here soon.
3. In 2011, the Santa Ana winds _____ (be) very strong.
4. _____ you ever _____ (be) to Griffith Park?
5. I _____ never _____ (have) a headache. I am really lucky.
6. When I lived in China, I _____ (visit) the Great Wall.
7. I _____ (live) in Los Angeles for one year. I still live in LA.
8. Michael Jackson _____ (raise) money for many charities.
9. Janet Jackson _____ (raise) money for many charities.
10. Janet Jackson _____ (graduate) from high school in 1984.
11. Janet Jackson _____ (appear) in the movie *For Colored Girls* in 2010.
12. Janet Jackson _____ (appear) in many movies.
13. Michael Jackson _____ (have) three children.
14. In March 2011, there _____ (be) an earthquake in Japan.
15. I _____ (watch) a movie in English last weekend.
16. I _____ (watch) many videos in English this week.

HOW OBSERVANT ARE YOU?

- **Oleg:** Have you seen a duck in Los Angeles?
- **Parvaneh:** Believe it or not, I have seen a duck in Los Angeles.
- **Oleg:** Where did you see it?
- **Parvaneh:** I saw it swimming in the pond on the university campus.

PRESENT PERFECT:
Ask your partner:
Have you seen . . .   ?

PAST:
Where did you see . . . ?
When did you see . . . ?

a crow _____

a hummingbird _____

a skunk _____

a lizard _____

a squirrel _____

solar panels _____

bamboo _____

a bird of paradise _____
(it's a flower)

a lily _____

an orange tree _____

IRREGULAR PAST TENSES

BASE	PAST	PARTICIPLE	BASE	PAST	PARTICIPLE
be	was /were	been	let (allow)	let	let
bear	bore	born	lie (posture)	lay	lain
beat	beat	beaten	light	lit/lighted	lit/lighted
become	became	become	lose	lost	lost
begin	began	begun	make	made	made
bend	bent	bent	mean	meant	meant
bet	bet	bet	meet	met	met
bite	bit	bitten	pay	paid	paid
bleed	bled	bled	prove	proved	proved/proven
blow	blew	blown	put	put	put
break	broke	broken	quit	quit	quit
breed	bred	bred	read	read	read
bring	brought	brought	ride	rode	ridden
build	built	built	ring	rang	rung
buy	bought	bought	rise	rose	risen
catch	caught	caught	run	ran	run
choose	chose	chosen	say	said	said
come	came	come	seek	sought	sought
cost	cost	cost	sell	sold	sold
creep	crept	crept	send	sent	sent
cut	cut	cut	set	set	set
deal	dealt	dealt	sew	sewed	sewed/sewn
dig	dug	dug	shake	shook	shaken
dive	dived/dove	dived	shine	shined/shone	shined/shone
do	did	done	shoot	shot	shot
draw	drew	drawn	shrink	shrank	shrunk
drink	drank	drunk	shut	shut	shut
drive	drove	driven	sing	sang	sung
eat	ate	eaten	sink	sank	sunk
fall	fell	fallen	sit	sat	sat
feed	fed	fed	sleep	slept	slept
feel	felt	felt	speak	spoke	spoken
fight	fought	fought	speed	sped	sped
find	found	found	spend	spent	spent
fly	flew	flown	spin	spun	spun
freeze	froze	frozen	spring	sprang	sprung
get	got	gotten/got	stand	stood	stood
give	gave	given	steal	stole	stolen
go	went	gone	stink	stank	stunk
grind	ground	ground	strike	struck	stricken/struck
grow	grew	grown	string	strung	strung
hang	hung/hanged	hung/hanged	sweep	swept	swept
have	had	had	swim	swam	swum
hear	heard	heard	take	took	taken
hide	hid	hidden	teach	taught	taught
hit	hit	hit	tear	tore	torn
hold	held	held	tell	told	told
hurt	hurt	hurt	think	thought	thought
keep	kept	kept	throw	threw	thrown
knit	knit/knitted	knit/knitted	wake	woke	woken/awakened
know	knew	known	wear	wore	worn
lay	laid	laid	weave	wove	woven
lead	led	led	weep	wept	wept
leave	left	left	win	won	won
lend	lent	lent	write	wrote	written

USING THE PRESENT PERFECT WITH: TODAY, THIS MORNING, THIS WEEK, THIS MONTH, THIS YEAR

- **Yelena:** How many times have you eaten out this week?
- **Roberto:** I don't usually eat in restaurants, but this week I have already eaten out twice.

Complete the questions with the correct form of the past participle for the present perfect tense (for irregular verbs, use the list on the previous page). Ask the questions and speak with your classmates.

1. How many phone calls have you _____ (make) this morning?

2. How many text messages have you _____ (send) today?

3. How many cups of coffee have you _____ (have) this week?

4. What have you _____ (see) in Los Angeles this month?

5. Who(m) have you _____ (speak) English to this week?

6. What have you _____ (do) at school this month?

7. How many videos have you _____ (see) this week?

8. How many movies have you _____ (see) this month?

9. How many books have you _____ (read) this year?

10. Where have you _____ (eat) this week?

11. How many kinds of fruit have you _____ (eat) this week?

12. How many friends have you _____ (make) this month?

13. How many hours have you _____ (speak) English today?

14. How many times have you _____ (shop) in a mall this month?

15. How many times have you _____ (ask) for directions this week?

16. What kind of music have you _____ (listen) to this week?

USING THE PRESENT PERFECT: HUMAN BINGO

LOSE YOUR WALLET : **Diana: Have** you ever **lost** your wallet?
POSSIBLE ANSWERS : **Xiao:** Yes, I **have lost** my wallet. In fact, I lost it last week.
Vyasheslav: No, I **have never lost** my wallet.

Ask your classmates questions in the present perfect using the following phrases. If a person says, "Yes," cross off that square and <u>change partners.</u> If a person says, "No," you may ask that person another question. When you have crossed off enough questions to make one vertical (|), horizontal (—), or diagonal line (\ ), say BINGO!
Remember to change the verb to the past participle (third form).

go surfing	walk on the Hollywood Walk of Fame	go hiking in Griffith Park	visit the Getty Center
go skiing	go bowling	go camping	go fishing
go dancing in LA	go sailing	drive a car in LA	see an actor or actress
dream in English	travel in Europe	bake a cake	visit the Gene Autry Western Heritage Museum

Focus on Sentence Structure: FOR or SINCE

- **Go Woon: Have** you **had** your dog long?
- **Xiaolan:** Not really. This is my friend's dog, but she's on vacation now. I **have taken** care of her dog **for about ten days**. No, wait. My friend left three weeks ago. That means **I've taken** care of him **since the first of the month**.

Use "for" with a period of time. |←——— ten days ———→|

Use "since" with a point in time   ● the first of the month
(on the clock or on the calendar)

Choose "for" or "since":

_____ April   _____ five months
_____ six minutes   _____ May 21st
_____ twelve weeks   _____ January
_____ 8:00 A.M.   _____ one second
_____ September 22nd   _____ Tuesday
_____ midnight   _____ seven years

Discuss the Timeline

The past tense is used for events that happen quickly and do not continue into the present. Sometimes another action or state begins then and continues into the present. You can use the present perfect for these states, but you must change the verb.

Look at the timeline and choose from verbs in the box to talk about Steve's life.
Structure: Steve has _____ since _____. / Steve has _____ for _____ years.

moved to LA	found a job	enrolled in school	bought a car	got a dog
2000	2005	2006	2009	2010

| had | study | live | own | work |

1. _____
2. _____
3. _____
4. _____
5. _____

SURVEY USING THE PRESENT PERFECT AND THE PAST

Keep track of every person's answers like this: 卌 |

Present Perfect Question:	Yes	No	NEXT: Past Tense Questions:
Have you ever seen a ghost? *Possible answers:* *Yes, I have.* *No, I haven't.*			When did you see it? Where did you see it? Were you afraid of it?
Have you ever seen a UFO (an unidentified flying object)?			When did you see it? Where did you see it? What did it look like?
Have you ever experienced ESP (extrasensory perception=you know something that you haven't seen, heard, smelled, tasted or felt)?			What happened?
Have you ever had a premonition (a feeling that you know something will happen in the future)?			What happened?
Have you ever seen a rattlesnake?			When did you see it? Where did you see it? What happened?
Have you ever seen a celebrity in person?			When did you see him/her? Where did you see him/her?
Have you ever attended a baseball game?			When did you attend the game? Where did you go to see it?

HAVE YOU EVER . . . ?

Diana: Have you ever **flown a kite**?
Xiao: Yes, I **have flown a kite.** (OR: No, **I haven't flown a kite.**)

On a piece of paper, write down something unusual that you have done in your life. You may get some ideas from the list or the pictures below:

been to Australia	raised a pet snake
built a desk	read a book in English
cooked for 50 people	repaired cars
grown tomatoes	ridden a camel
knit (or knitted) a sweater	roasted a turkey
painted a painting	run in a marathon
painted a room	sewn a dress
planted a tree	won a race
raised chickens	won money in a lottery

Without including your name, your teacher will write all of these unusual activities on the board. Then you will have to question your classmates to find out what they have done. Ask only yes/no questions!

been skydiving   gone hiking   been mountain climbing

flown a kite

FOCUS ON SENTENCE STRUCTURE: ADVERBS

ADJECTIVES	ADVERBS
Answer the question: **What** (kind of) . . . ? Modify nouns: adj. noun He is a <u>skillful</u> surfer. noun + linking verb + adjective He is skillful. SOME LINKING VERBS* "TO BE" (IS, AM, ARE, WAS, WERE) TO LOOK TO SOUND TO SMELL TO TASTE TO FEEL Example: She looks beautiful.	Answer the question: **How** (do you DO something) . . . ? Modify verbs: verb adverb He surfs <u>skillfully.</u>

- **Go Woon:** How do you surf?
- **Mario:** I'm not a good surfer, but **I surf carefully**. I am careful not to hit rocks, the pier, or my friends when I surf.

HOW TO MAKE ADVERBS FROM ADJECTIVES

WHEN MADE FROM MOST ADJECTIVES		WHEN MADE FROM ADJECTIVES THAT END IN "LE"		WHEN MADE FROM ADJECTIVES THAT END IN "Y"		EXCEPTIONS	
ADJECTIVE	ADVERB	ADJECTIVE	ADVERB	ADJECTIVE	ADVERB	ADJECTIVE	ADVERB
SLOW	SLOWLY	TERRIBLE	TERRIBLY	SLOPPY	SLOPPILY	FAST	FAST
BAD	BADLY	SIMPLE	SIMPLY	BUSY	BUSILY	HARD	HARD
						GOOD	WELL
						EARLY	EARLY
						LATE	LATE

GOOD & WELL

ADJECTIVE	ADVERB
GOOD	WELL
WELL (NOT SICK)	WELL

The question: "How do you feel?" uses the linking verb "feel" and needs an adjective. The correct answer: "Well" (not sick) —or— "Good" (not hot, cold, unhappy, or tired).

*These verbs can be used as linking verbs or action verbs. If they can be substituted with the verb "to be" without changing the meaning, you know that they are being used as linking verbs and therefore require adjectives.

AN EXERCISE ON ADVERBS AND ADJECTIVES

Circle the correct answer.

Example: He paints | sloppy (sloppily) |

1. She cooks | good   well. |

2. He sings | beautiful   beautifully. |

3. He is | intelligent   intelligently. |

4. She drives | fast   fastly. |

5. They paint | sloppy   sloppily. |

6. She is | beautiful   beautifully. |

7. You look | beautiful   beautifully. |

8. They type | accurate   accurately. |

9. She dresses | neat   neatly. |

10. Her dress is | neat   neatly. |

11. He checks his work | careful   carefully. |

12. She works | careless   carelessly. |

13. They were | careless   carelessly. |

36

FIND SOMEONE WHO:

You have to find people in this class who do activities as described in the questions. Go around the class to ask your classmates.

- **Mario:** How do you swim?
- **Go Woon:** I swim slowly.

Here are the rules of this game:
- If a person does not do the activity as described, do not write anything. Go to the next question.
- If a person does the activity as described, write the person's name in the blank *and change partners.*
- When you have found a person for each question, you have won!

You may ask in two ways:
- How do you _____? **HOW DO YOU SWIM?**
- Do you [verb] [adverb]? **DO YOU SWIM FAST?**

1. Find someone who swims fast. _____
2. Find someone who plays cards dishonestly. _____
3. Find someone who plays chess well. _____
4. Find someone who translates accurately from French to his/her language. _____
5. Find someone who works hard. _____
6. Find someone who eats slowly. _____
7. Find someone who sings beautifully. _____
8. Find someone who dances gracefully. _____
9. Find someone who plays tennis badly. _____
10. Find someone who plays Internet games well. _____
11. Find someone who paints sloppily. _____
12. Find someone who drives carefully. _____
13. Find someone who types fast. _____
14. Find someone who speaks softly. _____
15. Find someone who sews well. _____
16. Find someone who speaks Japanese well. _____
17. Find someone who studies hard. _____
18. Find someone who walks quickly. _____
19. Find someone who skates carelessly. _____
20. Find someone who plays basketball well. _____

REVIEW

Change the word given to make a correct sentence, or choose the word.

Example: Los Angeles is __more interesting__ (interesting) than New York.

1. Mathematics is as _____ (difficult) as history.
2. I've known my best friend _____ (for / since) ten years.
3. I still live in Los Angeles. I _____ (live) in Los Angeles a long time.
4. He drives _____ (careless / carelessly).
5. California is _____ (beautiful / beautifully).
6. She looks _____ (comfortable / comfortably).
7. I _____ (meet) Bob yesterday.
8. If you want to bake a cake, you need _____ (a / the / --) eggs.
9. _____ (a / the / --) best restaurant I know is on _____ (a / the / --) Reseda Boulevard.
10. Michael Jackson _____ (record) 11 solo albums.
11. Venice is the _____ (beautiful / more beautiful / most beautiful) city in the world.
12. I met my best friend _____ (in / for / since) 2011.
13. I have known my best friend _____ (in / for / since) 2011.
14. She eats _____ (slow / slowly).
15. I have to go to _____ (a / the / --) library for _____ (a / the / --) book.
16. He works _____ (hard / hardly).*
17. They _____ (visit) the Grand Canyon many times.
18. It was a delicious meal. It was _____ (good / well).
19. Jack and Jill are married now. They _____ (meet) five years ago.
20. Janet Jackson _____ (record) 10 albums.
21. Love is _____ (important) than money.
22. I moved from NY to LA. I _____ (live) in NY a long time.
23. That smells so _____ (good / well)!
24. He translates very _____ (accurate / accurately).
25. I have to go to _____ (a / the / --) supermarket.

*NOTE: There are similar adverbs. Don't get them confused.

    LATE = not on time   **LATELY** = recently
    HARD = with great effort   **HARDLY** = almost never

4. Let's Talk about the Bravest Celebrity

Elizabeth Taylor was known as a great beauty, an actress, and as a businesswoman. In the more than twenty years since it has been marketed, her perfume White Diamonds has earned over one billion dollars.

Few people know that in 1987, while she **was marketing** her perfume Passion, she visited HIV/AIDS patients in every city on her tour. At that time, many people did not understand that AIDS could not be caught from touching or being near sick people. It was very unpopular to support AIDS, and people did not even want to write the word "AIDS" on a check for a charity. Elizabeth Taylor changed all of that.

When her friend Rock Hudson **was dying** of AIDS in 1985, he was too ashamed of the disease to admit he had it. His death inspired her to start the National AIDS Research Foundation. She was not

FEBRUARY 27, 1932 – MARCH 23, 2011

afraid of public opinion. Suddenly, with Elizabeth's celebrity behind the cause, people started contributing to the foundation and reporters started writing about it.

In 1990, she visited Congress to help pass a law that prevents discrimination against people with HIV. She sent perfumed lavender notes to senators and congressional representatives asking them to read information on HIV. When she called members of Congress, they all spoke to her. They were happy to be speaking to such a beautiful actress, and she used her power very effectively.

Elizabeth Taylor had seven husbands, four children, and many friends. On September 11, 2001, Elizabeth Taylor **was visiting** her friend Michael Jackson in New York City. The great actor Marlon Brando **was staying** in Michael's hotel, and both he and Elizabeth had attended Michael's two concerts on September 7 and 10. These stars usually travel by air, but on September 11, after the terrorist attack on the World Trade Center, no planes **were flying.** Some people say that while others were terrified, Elizabeth was not afraid. She stayed in the city to help people.

Michael Jackson and Elizabeth Taylor became very close friends. She said, "He had one of the worst childhoods ever. I think I had the second."

Elizabeth Taylor was not afraid to speak up for what she believed. Her son, Christopher Wilding, said that Elizabeth taught him "to be expansive with compassion and generosity, to be open-minded and fair. She taught this entirely by example."

Reading Comprehension

1. What was Elizabeth Taylor doing in 1987?
2. Why was supporting HIV/AIDS charities unpopular in 1985?
3. How did Elizabeth Taylor use her celebrity?
4. What happened in 1990?
5. What did Elizabeth Taylor teach her son, Christopher Wilding?

CRITICAL THINKING

1. It takes bravery to support unpopular causes. Can you think of any unpopular causes in our world today? Can you think of any problems in our world today that people do not want to talk about or think about?
2. What are the most important lessons your parents taught you? What would you like to pass on to your children or the next generation? Why?

SPEAK ABOUT SOMEONE YOU ADMIRE (write about 250 words in preparation)

Prepare to speak about someone you admire who is still alive.. Tell the class what this person did (past) and has done (present perfect), and how he or she does things (adverbs).

Getting Caught in the Act (of Doing Something)

PAST CONTINUOUS:
Subject + **was/were** + **verb+ing**.

- **Mario:** What **were** you do**ing** at 5:00 yesterday afternoon?
- **Sarah:** I **was** bak**ing** cookies with my daughter.

| PAST CONTINUOUS | at 5:00 yesterday or: when the telephone rang | We are studying English now. PRESENT CONTINUOUS | FUTURE CONTINUOUS |

I was baking cookies at 5:00 yesterday.   I will be roasting a turkey at 6:00 tomorrow.

Before (and possibly after) 5:00 P.M., Sarah was baking cookies. When the telephone rang, she was baking cookies. Her baking was interrupted by the telephone call.

The past continuous expresses a CONTINUOUS action that was interrupted by another action or was IN PROGRESS at a particular time.

AN EXERCISE ON THE PAST CONTINUOUS

Speak with your partner:
1. What were you doing at 11:00 last night? _____
2. What were you doing at 4:00 yesterday afternoon? _____
3. What were you doing when you heard that Michael Jackson had died?
   _____
4. What were you doing when you heard about the earthquake in Japan? _____
   _____
5. What were you doing ***all morning*** last Saturday? _____
6. What were you doing ***all afternoon*** last Sunday? _____

Ask your partner some questions:
7. What _____ ?
8. What _____ ?
9. What _____ ?
10. What _____ ?

REVIEW
Circle the correct answer.

1. Elizabeth Taylor was the (courageous / more courageous / most courageous) celebrity.
2. She was (brave / more brave / braver) than other celebrities.
3. She was as (famous / more famous / most famous) as Marlon Brando.
4. She did not have the (good / better / best) childhood.
5. She (has appeared / appeared) in many movies.
6. At 9:00 yesterday evening, I (have watched / watched / was watching) television.
7. It is dangerous to drive (fast / fastly / quick / slow).
8. My friend lives in (a / the / ---) United States now. He (lives / lived / has lived) here (for / since) six years.
9. (A / the / ---) gold is (expensive / most expensive / more expensive) than (a / the/ ---) silver.
10. That soccer player really plays (good / well).

REVIEW QUESTION STRUCTURES
DID   DO   DOES   HAVE   HAS   IS   WAS   WILL

1. What _____ she doing when the boss came in?
2. What _____ she do yesterday?
3. What _____ she going to do tomorrow?
4. What _____ she done this week?
5. What _____ she do tomorrow?

WHAT WERE THEY DOING WHEN THE PLANE ARRIVED?

These people were waiting for an airplane to take them from Los Angeles to New York, but their airplane was delayed due to stormy weather. They were waiting for a long time, and they were keeping themselves busy. Finally, their airplane arrived. What were they and some airport employees doing when their airplane arrived?

42

Write your sentences here to describe the picture. Use the past continuous. Describe what was happening when the plane arrived.

1. **Example:** *He was working when the plane arrived.*
2.
3.
4.
5.
6.
7.
8.
9.
10.
11.
12.
13.
14.
15.
16.
17.
18.
19.
20.

FOCUS ON QUESTIONS

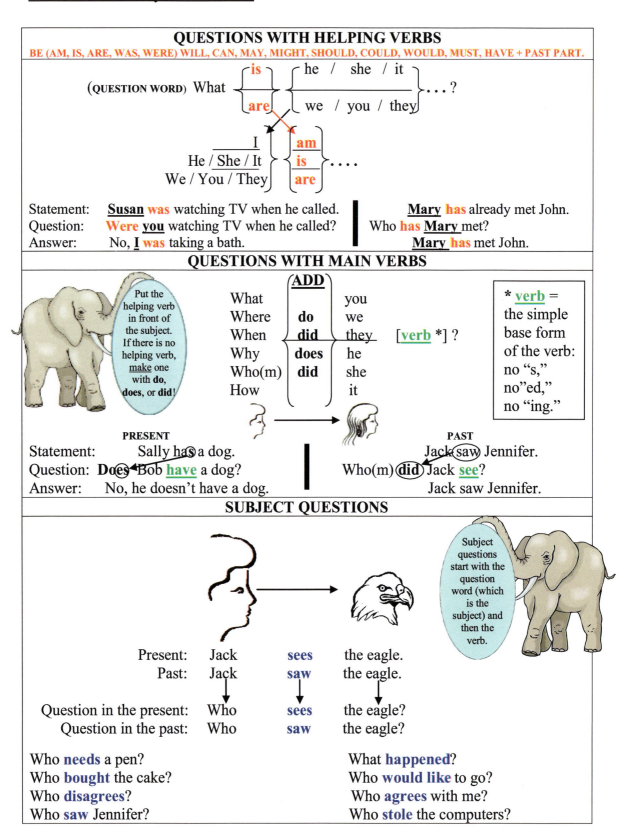

QUESTIONS WITH HELPING VERBS
BE (AM, IS, ARE, WAS, WERE) WILL, CAN, MAY, MIGHT, SHOULD, COULD, WOULD, MUST, HAVE + PAST PART.

(QUESTION WORD) What { is / are } { he / she / it / we / you / they } ... ?

I — am
He / She / It — is
We / You / They — are ...

Statement: <u>Susan</u> **was** watching TV when he called.
Question: **Were** <u>you</u> watching TV when he called?
Answer: No, **I was** taking a bath.

<u>Mary</u> **has** already met John.
Who **has** <u>Mary</u> met?
<u>Mary</u> **has** met John.

QUESTIONS WITH MAIN VERBS

Put the helping verb in front of the subject. If there is no helping verb, <u>make</u> one with **do**, **does**, or **did**!

What / Where / When / Why / Who(m) / How { ADD do / did / does / did } { you / we / they / he / she / it } [verb *] ?

* **verb** = the simple base form of the verb: no "s," no "ed," no "ing."

PRESENT
Statement: Sally **has** a dog.
Question: **Does** Bob **have** a dog?
Answer: No, he doesn't have a dog.

PAST
Jack **saw** Jennifer.
Who(m) **did** Jack **see**?
Jack saw Jennifer.

SUBJECT QUESTIONS

Subject questions start with the question word (which is the subject) and then the verb.

Present: Jack **sees** the eagle.
Past: Jack **saw** the eagle.

Question in the present: Who **sees** the eagle?
Question in the past: Who **saw** the eagle?

Who **needs** a pen?
Who **bought** the cake?
Who **disagrees**?
Who **saw** Jennifer?

What **happened**?
Who **would like** to go?
Who **agrees** with me?
Who **stole** the computers?

MORE REVIEW OF QUESTION STRUCTURES
Choose the correct form.

1. I couldn't find you. _____
    a. Where you went?
    b. Where do you went?
    c. Where did you go?
    d. Where have you went?
2. I like your friend. _____
    a. How long you known him?
    b. How long did you known him?
    c. How long have you know him?
    d. How long have you known him?
3. _____ when you met her?
    a. What she was wearing
    b. What was she wearing
    c. What she wearing
    d. What was she wore
4. What do you think? _____
    a. Solar power better for the environment than nuclear power?
    b. Solar power is better for the environment than nuclear power?
    c. Is better for the environment solar power than nuclear power?
    d. Is solar power better for the environment than nuclear power?
5. So you want to borrow my car. _____
    a. How you drive?
    b. How have you drive?
    c. How do you drive?
    d. How's you drive?
6. Jack was drunk last night. _____
    a. Who drove him home?
    b. Who did drive him home?
    c. Who has drove him home?
    d. Who was drive him home?
7. I heard it was a great party. _____
    a. Who(m) you met?
    b. Who(m) did you met?
    c. Who(m) did you meet?
    d. Who(m) do you met?
8. Bob is cute. _____
    a. Do he has a girlfriend?
    b. Did he has a girlfriend?
    c. Does he a girlfriend?
    d. Does he have a girlfriend?

ASK QUESTIONS. WITH A PARTNER, MAKE QUESTIONS, ASK AND ANSWER THEM.

QUESTIONS IN THE PRESENT TENSE (EVERY DAY, EVERY WEEK, EVERY MONTH, ETC.)

- **Ana:** Where do you usually go to eat?
- **Jack:** There are so many good restaurants. What kind of food do you like?

1. What – eat – in the evening _____
2. What kind of music – you – like _____
3. Where – you – go dancing _____

QUESTIONS IN THE SIMPLE PAST TENSE

- **Ana:** Who(m) did you meet yesterday?
- **Jack:** Did you see me with anybody? Did you spy on me?

4. How far – walk – yesterday _____
5. Who – talk to – last night _____
6. Where – stay – last week _____

QUESTIONS IN THE PRESENT CONTINUOUS/PRESENT PROGRESSIVE (NOW)

- **Ana:** What is your brother doing now?
- **Jack:** Aren't you watching him? He's surfing.

7. Where – your friend – go _____
8. What Internet game – you – play _____
9. Who(m) – you – call _____

QUESTIONS WITH THE MODALS (CAN, MAY, WILL, MIGHT, SHOULD, COULD, MUST)

- **Ana:** Can you recommend a good restaurant near here?
- **Jack:** There are so many good restaurants. Should I recommend a Chinese restaurant?

10. Can – help me – carry my luggage _____
11. Will – rain – tomorrow _____
12. Where – should – go _____

CONVERSATION: AMERICAN STYLE

- **Ana:** Do you like this music?
- **Jack:** Yes.
- **Dong:** Yes, I do. I'm a big fan of jazz and Wynton Marsalis. I attended his concert in Beijing in 2000.
- **Ana:** I didn't know Wynton Marsalis performed in China. Can you tell me about it?

Whom do you think Ana will want to talk to: Dong or Jack? When first meeting people, even ten seconds without speaking will make many Americans nervous unless they really know their conversation partner. In some Asian countries, a pause in the conversation is a sign of respect because the listener is thinking about what was just said. Not so in America! You can keep the conversation going by asking questions.

PRACTICE: Try speaking continually with your partner for ten minutes, no pauses.

DO YOU HAVE AN ALIBI*?

Last night someone stole four computers from the computer lab. The crime happened sometime between 6:00 and 11:00 P.M. The director thinks someone from our class stole the computers because the video camera in the lab recorded students carrying out the computers. They look like students in our class. The director is too busy to question everyone, so we have to interrogate the suspects.

Four students are suspects. They have to leave the classroom. They say they have an alibi: Two say they went to a restaurant together, and the other two say they watched a movie and did some shopping at the mall. The pairs have a few minutes to talk together to make sure their stories are the same.

The other students have some detective work to do. They have to write very DETAILED questions for the suspects. They will question each member of each pair separately. If each member of the pair has the same story, they are telling the truth. If their stories are different, they are lying about where they were. They stole the computers! (It is very important to keep the students of each pair separate once the questioning begins so that they cannot exchange information.)

Write some questions. Try to be very DETAILED in your questioning so that we will be able to know who the liars are.
<u>Remember to use the past continuous. Example: What were you doing at 7:00 P.M.?</u>

Questions for Suspect #1 NAME: **The Restaurant**	**Questions for Suspect #2 NAME:** **The Mall and the Movie**
<u>Examples:</u> *Were you served by a waiter or a waitress? What did he/she look like? What was he/she wearing?* 	

*An alibi is proof that you are innocent because you were in another place when there was a crime.

Questions for Suspect #3 NAME: The Restaurant	Questions for Suspect #4 NAME: The Mall and the Movie

CONCLUSIONS: WHO STOLE THE COMPUTERS?

Did suspects #1 and #3 have the same story?
How did their stories differ?

_____
_____
_____

Did suspects #2 and #4 have the same story?
How did their stories differ?

_____
_____
_____

5. Let's Give Advice

What does a mother-in-law do? She gives advice.
She's not your mother, so she can't tell you what you HAVE TO do.
She doesn't have power, and she knows it. All she can do is give advice.

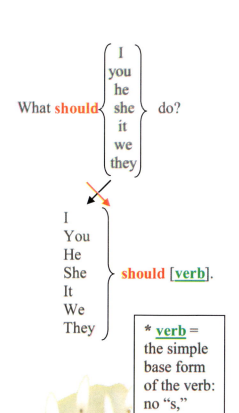

* **verb** = the simple base form of the verb: no "s," no "ed," no "ing."

Mother-in-law: Jack is getting thinner. I think he has lost his appetite.
Lucy: That's because he's working out. He's—
Mother-in-law: He loves my soup. He can't resist my soup. You **should use** my recipe.
Lucy: He's on a diet. He doesn't want—
Mother-in-law: I have an idea! His birthday is coming up. You **should bake** him a cake.
Lucy: But—
Mother-in-law: That **should fatten** him up. Don't make a chocolate cake. It's bad for his skin. You **should bake** a lemon cake.
Lucy: He said he doesn't want me to bake him a cake.
Mother-in-law: Really? *I* **should bake** him a cake. I know he loves *my* cakes.
Lucy: But he's on a diet!
Mother-in-law: He **shouldn't go** on a diet! He's too thin!

Mothers-in-law are not the only ones who give advice. We ALL give advice. We even ask for advice: What should I do? What should I eat? How should I study?

Discuss these problems with your partner and give advice using "should."
You ask:
1. I can't sleep at night. What should I do?
2. I don't know how to use the bus system. What should I do?
3. My friend wants to borrow my best dress. What should I do?
4. I feel nervous. What should I do?
5. I feel bored. What should I do?

Your partner asks:
6. I don't like to eat alone, but my friends are busy. What should I do?
7. I want to meet Americans. What should I do?
8. I'm lonely. What should I do?
9. I can't understand the assigned videos. What should I do?
10. I want to learn English fast. What should I do?

Tell the class: What is the best advice you received from your partner?

MORE ADVICE – MORE DISCUSSION
Ask your classmates for advice and give them advice.
Present your best ideas to the class.

1. I forgot my key inside my room. What should I do?
2. I don't have enough money to pay the bills. What should I do?
3. I am spending too much money on food. What should I do?
4. It's cold inside the classroom, but it's hot outside. What should I wear?
5. My friends never speak English but I want to speak English. What should I do?
6. I overslept and if I go to class I will be late. Should I arrive late or stay home?
7. I lost my textbook. What should I do?
8. My friend is trying to quit smoking and doesn't want to be near cigarettes. Should I stop smoking when I am with my friend?
9. My friend is on a diet. Should I bake a cake?
10. A dog followed me home. What should I do?
11. My roommate just bought a cat. I am allergic to cats. What should I do?
12. I am hungry and I don't have any money in my pocket. What should I do?
13. I lost my cell phone. What should I do?
14. My friend is drunk. My friend is planning to drive us home. I know my friend should not drive. I should drive us home, but I don't know how to drive. What should I do?
15. My friend is driving. The speed limit is 65 miles per hour, but my friend is going 80. Should I say anything to my friend?

HELP FOR AN ADVICE COLUMNIST

An **advice** columnist is a journalist who answers readers' letters about their problems and **writes his** or her recommendations in a daily or a weekly column in the newspaper.

Ms. Ida Smith is an advice columnist for *The Tinseltown Daily* and she is extremely busy. In fact, she's swamped! She has so many readers' letters that she can't handle them all. She would like our help. Here are some of the letters she has just received. Discuss them with your partner and come up with some good advice. After reading and discussing all the letters, decide which one is the most important and present your advice to the class. Remember to use "should."

April 30, 20--

Dear Ida,

I live with a roommate. She always eats my food out of the refrigerator. She never buys food. It is getting expensive. What should I do?

Sincerely,
Starving Student

April 30, 20--

Dear Ms. Smith,

I am 14 years old. All my friends wear makeup, but my mother doesn't want me to wear any. What should I do?

Sincerely,
Unhappy Teenager

April 30, 20--

Dear Ms. Ida Smith,

I think my best friend is stealing money from me. We live together, so it is difficult to protect my money. What should I do?

Sincerely,
Angry Roommate

April 30, 20--

Dear Ida,

My boyfriend left me two months ago. I miss him. My parents and friends do not really understand how unhappy I am. I am not hungry, but I eat constantly. I gained 10 pounds. What should I do?

Love,
Sad Ex-girlfriend

April 30, 20--

Dear Ms. Smith,

I took my girlfriend home to meet my family. She drank too much vodka and got drunk. She said some terrible things to my mother. What should I do?

Sincerely,
Embarrassed Boyfriend

April 30, 20--

Dear Ida,

    I am taking care of a very expensive cat for a friend who is on vacation. The cat died yesterday. I don't have enough money to buy another cat for my friend. What should I do?

    Sincerely,
    Panicked Friend

April 30, 20--

Dear Ms. Smith,

    Our neighbors bought a very large dog that barks all night. I talked to them about it, but the dog continues to bark. What should I do? My neighbor is also an important man in the police department.

    Sincerely,
    Sleepless Neighbor

April 30, 20--

Dear Ida,

    I live with two other students in an apartment. Each of us should clean the apartment once every three weeks. I always clean the apartment when it is my turn, but the others never clean. I talk to them about this every week, but they won't listen to me. What should I do?

    Sincerely,
    Over-worked Student

Never use "to" with "should." "Should" is followed by a simple verb: no "s" and no "ing."

SURVEY USING "SHOULD"

Keep track of every person's answers like this: ||||| |

Question:	Yes	No
Should all cars be required to have high miles per gallon?		
Notes:		
Should the TOEFL or IELTS test be required for university students?		
Notes:		
Should children be required to eat 5 fruits and/or vegetables per day?		
Notes:		
Should all new buildings be required to have solar panels?		
Notes:		
Should smoking be allowed in parks and on university campuses?		
Notes:		

REVIEW THE PRESENT PERFECT WITH:
FOR (A PERIOD OF TIME)
SINCE (A POINT IN TIME)

Complete the questions with the correct form of the present perfect and the correct form of the past participle. Ask the questions and speak with your classmates.

1. What have you _____ (see) in Los Angeles since you arrived in the U.S.?

2. Who(m) have you _____ (meet) in Los Angeles since you arrived in the U.S.?

3. What have you _____ (buy) since you arrived in the U.S.?

4. Have you _____ (eat) anything strange since you arrived in the U.S.?

5. Have you _____ (see) anything surprising since you arrived in the U.S.?

6. Have you _____ (watch) television since you arrived in the U.S.?

7. Has your computer _____ (crash) since you bought it?

8. Has your computer _____ (get) infected with a virus since you bought it?

9. Have you _____ (be) sick since you arrived in the U.S.?

    The following questions may be answered with:
    - Yes, I have _____ for . . . .
    - No, I have never _____ for . . . .

10. Have you ever _____ (speak) English for twenty-four hours straight (not counting time for sleeping)?

11. Have you ever _____ (stay) up for twenty-four hours straight (no sleep)?

12. Have you ever _____ (stop) eating for twenty-four hours straight?

13. Have you ever _____ (dance) for three hours?

14. Have you ever _____ (drive) a car for eight hours without a break?

15. Have you ever _____ (jog) for two hours without a break?

6. Let's Talk about the Lottery

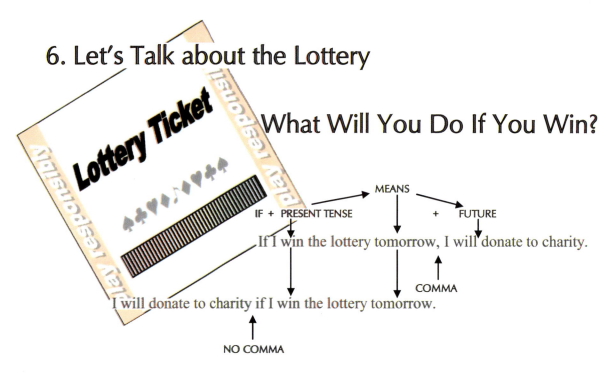

What Will You Do If You Win?

IF + PRESENT TENSE + FUTURE (MEANS)

If I win the lottery tomorrow, I will donate to charity. (COMMA)

I will donate to charity if I win the lottery tomorrow. (NO COMMA)

Crazy English! All of the following time expressions are followed by the present tense, even when speaking about the future:
- **after**
- **as soon as**
- **before**
- **if**
- **until**
- **when**
- **while**

Use one of the above time expressions to fill in the blanks:
1. You will have to get a license _____ you can drive a car.
2. I am waiting for you. Hurry! We will go _____ you are ready.
3. He is going to continue taking the test _____ he passes.
4. They will not take drugs or drink alcohol _____ they are training as athletes.
5. _____ you go sightseeing in LA, you will have a great time.
6. _____ she graduates from the university, she will find a job.
7. _____ I see a falling star, I will make a wish.
8. _____ it rains, I always carry an umbrella.

Who is the most generous person in this class?

What will you do if _____ gives you $1,000,000.00?

Critical Thinking: Which is the best charitable cause? Why?

OPTIMISM AND PESSIMISM: WHAT MIGHT HAPPEN?

Consider "what might happen if . . . ." and make up a story with your classmates. It can be an optimistic story (you imagine that great things will happen) or a pessimistic story (you imagine that terrible things will happen).
For example:
    I want to bake a cake this afternoon, but I know I shouldn't.
    If I bake a cake this afternoon, I will eat the whole cake.
    If I eat the whole cake, I will get fat.
    If I get fat, I will have to buy new clothes.
    If I have to buy new clothes, I will have to take money out of my bank account.
    If I take money out of my bank account, I will not be able to pay the rent.
    If I can't pay the rent, my landlord will evict me.
    If my landlord evicts me, I will have to sleep in the park.
    If I sleep in the park, I will get sick.
    If I get sick, I will die.
    So . . . I am not going to bake a cake this afternoon.

Start with any idea. Here are some ideas:
If I don't practice English, ...
If I stay up too late playing Internet games, ...
If I speak impolitely to people, ...
If I don't call my parents, ...

USING "IF"+"WILL" TO DISCUSS POSSIBILITIES

On the following page, you will see some pictures. They show a man climbing up a path in the Santa Monica Mountains between Los Angeles and the San Fernando Valley. He has a problem. He lives in an isolated area with no roads and no public transportation. He wants to attend his neighbor's birthday party, and he plans to give his neighbor a chicken and a bag of grain to feed the chicken. It is a dangerous area, and only one path leads to his friend's home. Whenever traveling on this path, he has to take his dog with him to protect him from mountain lions (sometimes called cougars).

He has a big problem. The path is so narrow that he can carry only one thing at a time.

If he leaves the chicken alone with the bag of grain, the chicken will peck through the bag and eat the grain.

If he leaves the dog alone with the chicken, the dog will eat the chicken.

How can he reach his destination and not lose anything?

Discuss the problem with your partner and put the pictures in the order that will enable him to arrive at his friend's house with his dog, the chicken, and the bag of grain.

Photo by K. Fink — A Mountain Lion

SURVEY USING "IF + WILL"

Keep track of every person's answers like this: |||| |

Question:	Yes	No
If you find a wallet with $100 in it, will you take it to the lost and found?		
Notes:		
If you see another student cheating during a test, will you tell the teacher?		
Notes:		
If you hate your sister's (or brother's) fiancé (or fiancée), will you tell your sister or brother?		
Notes:		
If your best friend's boyfriend/girlfriend is going out with other women/men, will you tell him or her?		
Notes:		
If the clerk at a grocery store forgets to charge you for an expensive item, will you tell him or her?		
Notes:		
If your friend asks you to tell a lie for him/her, will you do it?		
Notes:		
If your friend commits a crime, will you tell the police?		

FIND SUPERSTITIONS USING "IF + WILL"

Walk around the school or your neighborhood to interview people. Ask, "Excuse me. I'm a student. I am researching superstitions. Could you tell me a superstition?"

Example of a superstition: If you break a mirror,	you **will have** seven years of bad luck.
1) If ,	
2) If ,	
3) If ,	
4) If ,	
5) If ,	
6) If ,	
7) If ,	
8) If ,	
9) If ,	
10) If ,	
11) If ,	
12) If ,	
13) If ,	
14) If ,	
15) If ,	
16) If ,	
17) If ,	
18) If ,	
19) If ,	
20) If ,	

7. Let's Talk about Obligations, Rules and Regulations

Never use "to" with "must." "Must" is followed by a simple verb: no "s" and no "ing."

- **Natasha:** What's the problem, officer?
- **Policewoman:** You're not wearing a seatbelt. I **have to give** you a ticket.
- **Natasha:** I'll wear a seatbelt from now on.
- **Policewoman:** Good. You **must wear** a seatbelt at all times. But **I've** still **got to give** you a ticket.

MUST =

HAVE TO =

HAVE GOT TO

Some people argue that "must" is stronger than "have to." It might seem stronger because we don't use it very often. When we use "must," people really listen. However, they all mean the same thing.

- You must wear a seatbelt. =
- You have to wear a seatbelt. =
- You've got to wear a seatbelt.

If you don't, you will get a ticket! You will have to pay a lot of money!

PRESENT TENSE	PAST TENSE
I must go to the doctor. I have to go to the doctor. I have got to go to the doctor.	I had to go to the doctor

62

Rules and Regulations

TRAFFIC REGULATIONS	
What must you do?	What mustn't you do?
Ex.: You must drive carefully.	You must not drink and drive.

FAMILY RULES	
What must you do?	What mustn't you do?

RULES FOR YOUR DORM (DORMITORY) OR APARTMENT BUILDING	
What must you do?	What mustn't you do?

Vocabulary for the following page:

to arrest=to take to prison
collar=something around the neck
fine=money you pay for a mistake
to fine=to give you a ticket that you must pay for making a mistake
handicapped=not able to physically or mentally do what most people do

illegal=not permitted; against the law
leash=a long chain or rope, attached to a collar, used to walk or keep a dog
litter=garbage or paper on the street
to litter=to throw garbage or paper on the street
tag=a small hanging piece or note
taxes=money paid to the government

Work in pairs. One of you will be the policeman or policewoman. Ask each other the following questions. There are no answers given. You must think of your own answers.

QUESTIONS FOR YOU TO ASK THE POLICEMAN OR POLICEWOMAN

1. What will you do if I drive too fast?
2. What will you do if I park in a handicapped zone (blue zone)?
3. What will you do if I litter near the Los Angeles River?
4. What will you do if I throw garbage onto the freeway?
5. What will you do if someone steals my car?
6. What will you do if you see someone using illegal drugs?
7. What will you do if I steal money from a bank?
8. What will you do if I take my dog for a walk without a leash?
9. What will you do if I copy and sell movies on DVDs?
10. What will you do if I smoke in the classroom?
11. What will you do if I don't pay my taxes?

ANSWER IN COMPLETE SENTENCES! IF . . . .

QUESTIONS FOR THE POLICEMAN OR POLICEWOMAN TO ASK

1. What will happen if you don't have a collar and name tags on your dog?
2. What will happen if you don't put a leash on your dog?
3. What will happen to LA if everyone litters?
4. What will happen if you drink alcohol on the street?
5. What will probably happen if you don't stop at a stop sign?
6. What will probably happen if you drink and drive?
7. What will your parents (or husband or wife) say if you come home very late?
8. What will you say if I (as a policeman or woman) stop you for driving too fast?
9. What will you say if I (as a policeman or woman) tell you not to smoke outside near the door of this building?
10. What will your girlfriend (or wife) / boyfriend (or husband) say if she/he sees you with another man/woman?
11. What might happen if you don't wear a seatbelt in your car?

ANSWER IN COMPLETE SENTENCES! IF . . . .

ASK QUESTIONS WITH "MUST" AND "HAVE TO"

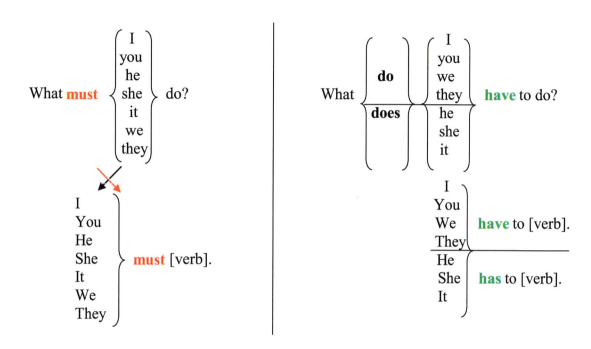

Ask each other questions using "must." Discuss.
1. If I want to enter an American university, what _____?
2. If my sister wants to come to Los Angeles, what _____?
3. If my brother wants to lose weight, what _____?
4. If Susan wants more friends, what _____?
5. If we want to save money, what _____?
6. If I want to be a good athlete, what _____?
7. If my friends want to pick fruit, where _____?
8. If I want to speak English well, what _____?
9. If I want to travel abroad, what _____?
10. If I want to meet Americans, what _____?

Ask each other questions using "have to." Discuss.
1. If I want to learn how to drive, what _____?
2. If my brother wants to take care of his teeth, what _____?
3. If we want to stay healthy, what _____?
4. If we want to meet people who speak English, what _____?
5. If I want to be a doctor, what _____?
6. If my sister wants to be a pilot, what _____?
7. If we want to stop using fossil fuels, what _____?
8. If I want to learn how to read better, what _____?
9. If I want to be a good student, what _____?
10. If a rattlesnake bites me, what _____?

MUST NOT ≠ DON'T HAVE TO

"Must not" is ***not*** the same as "don't have to." A different part of the sentence is negative, so there is a different meaning.

- **Mario:** How do you like your new job?
- **Roberto:** It's better than my last job as a waiter. I'm happy I **don't have to wear** a uniform, but there are a lot of dos and don'ts. I have to wear a suit and tie every day, and I **mustn't eat** or even snack at my desk.

MUST NOT
(DO NOT)

People must not smoke inside buildings.
Do not smoke!

DON'T HAVE TO
(IT'S OKAY, BUT IT'S NOT NECESSARY)

Women teachers don't have to wear dresses.
If a teacher wears a dress, it's great—
but it's not necessary.

Fill in the blanks with "must not" or "don't have to."

1) Near a school, you _____ drive faster than 25 miles per hour when there are children.

2) In Los Angeles, you _____ buy a car. You can use the bus.

3) If you are allergic to dairy foods, you _____ drink milk.

4) If you are a student at our school, you _____ wear uniform.

5) Women teachers _____ wear dresses at our school.

6) Men teachers _____ wear ties at our school.

7) In Los Angeles, you _____ litter.

8) In Los Angeles, you _____ take your dog out without a leash.

9) If you are rich, you _____ work.

10) If you drink a lot of alcohol, you _____ drive a car.

REVIEW: REQUIREMENTS

Work with your partner or partners to come up with the best ideas for the following goals. When you think you have enough good ideas, tell your teacher. Share these ideas with the class.

IF YOU WANT A PROMOTION, YOU		
must/have to . . .	must not . . .	don't have to . . .
1. _____	1. _____	1. _____
2. _____	2. _____	2. _____
3. _____	3. _____	3. _____
4. _____	4. _____	4. _____
5. _____	5. _____	5. _____

IF YOU WANT TO LEARN ENGLISH FAST, YOU		
must/have to . . .	must not . . .	don't have to . . .
1. _____	1. _____	1. _____
2. _____	2. _____	2. _____
3. _____	3. _____	3. _____
4. _____	4. _____	4. _____
5. _____	5. _____	5. _____

IF YOU WANT A LOT OF FRIENDS, YOU		
must/have to . . .	must not . . .	don't have to . . .
1. _____	1. _____	1. _____
2. _____	2. _____	2. _____
3. _____	3. _____	3. _____
4. _____	4. _____	4. _____
5. _____	5. _____	5. _____

REVIEW ASKING FOR ADVICE – USE SHOULD

Ask your classmates for advice, and give them advice.

1. I'm bored. What should I do?

2. I want to meet more people. What should I do?

3. I left my books in my last classroom. What should I do?

4. I found a gold ring on campus. What should I do?

5. I have a stomachache. What should I do?

6. My computer crashed. What should I do?

7. I forgot a classmate's name. What should I do?

8. I saw a cockroach in the kitchen. What should I do?

9. My friend invited me over for dinner. She is going to cook fish and broccoli. I hate fish and broccoli. What should I do?

10. A friend is going to come to visit. My friend just told me that she is a vegetarian. What should I feed her?

11. I'm preparing to go to a fancy party. I just realized my friend bought a dress exactly like mine. What should I wear?

12. A friend wants to give me a puppy. I'm not sure if I have enough time to take care of a puppy. What should I do?

13. My roommate likes to read late at night. The light bothers me and I can't fall asleep. What should I do?

14. A friend just called and said he is coming to visit me. He will be here in a few minutes. My apartment is really messy. What should I do?

15. My friend came to visit and left her cell phone. What should I do?

16. My friend came over to study with me but is only talking. What should I do?

CRITICAL THINKING: WHO DESERVES A PROMOTION?

You are managers in an import/export company and you need to promote **one** of your employees to the position of supervisor. Whom should you choose? Why?

Rose. She speaks English, Japanese, and two Indian languages. She is the office expert on our database, although she works very slowly. She often works during the lunch break, and skips lunch to get her work done. She has two small children and, due to their schedule, always arrives 15 minutes late to work. She has worked 6 years with this company.

Philip. He speaks English, Spanish, and Chinese. No one has asked him to train new workers, but he always takes them under his wing and helps them. He works fast and carefully, and everyone loves him. He gets his work done, but often comes late and leaves early because he has to take care of his sick mother. He has worked 4 years with this company.

Mildred. She speaks English, Spanish, and Korean. She gets along well with everyone and she has been able to get clients to sign contracts when no one else could. Last year these contracts were worth millions of dollars for us. She works very slowly and inaccurately on the computer and doesn't like to learn new skills. She has worked only 2 years with this company.

Daniel. He is an American citizen, but grew up in Brazil. He speaks English, Portuguese, and Spanish, and is studying Chinese at a night school. Although he has worked only 3 years with our company, he is an expert on how we do business. He works quickly and accurately. Although he speaks politely, no one likes him because everyone is envious of his knowledge.

Jill. She speaks English, French, Spanish, and Chinese. She is a computer geek and does her computer work very efficiently, but doesn't communicate very clearly. Although she has been with our company only 2 years, she got her father, an important manufacturer in Australia, to do business with us. We might lose her father as a client if we don't keep her happy.

Bob. He speaks English, Spanish, and Russian. He is the only one in the company who is willing to work overtime to solve problems, and he does this almost weekly. He works carefully and very accurately. He knows something about every department in our company. He speaks impolitely and everyone is afraid of him. Some customers hate him. He has worked 15 years with us.

Lisa. She speaks English, Korean, and Japanese. Our clients love her, and she works very efficiently and accurately. She speaks politely, dresses neatly, and does her job perfectly. However, she often suffers from headaches and is frequently absent due to health problems, and sometimes sleeps at her desk. She has worked 10 years with our company.

THIS EXERCISE MAY BE REPEATED AS: WHOM SHOULD WE LAY OFF? WHY?

8. Let's Talk about Our Activities
Get, Do, Take, and Make

GET	DO	TAKE	MAKE
a cold	a favor	a bath	a cake (all food)
along with someone	business	a shower	a complaint
home	exercises	a person out	a mistake
sick	homework	(for dinner, etc.)	a reservation
the flu	research	a pill	friends
tired	the dishes	care	money
to school, to work	the shopping	medicine	sure
upset	work	photographs	the bed
		time	up your mind

Fill in the blanks with the correct word.

1. Do you know how to _____ a delicious dinner?
2. I would like to _____ you out to dinner.
3. When you go abroad, you should _____ a lot of photos.
4. My neighbors are noisy. I am going to _____ a complaint.
5. He's not friendly. He doesn't _____ along with anyone.
6. Could you _____ me a favor? Please help me change a tire.
7. She's very popular. She can _____ friends easily.
8. Your room looks terrible. You should _____ your bed.
9. Be careful. Don't _____ any mistakes on this exercise.
10. I usually _____ home late.
11. You should _____ sure you have your keys before you close the door.
12. If I work very hard, I usually _____ tired.
13. Did you _____ your homework last night?
14. When I have a headache, I _____ a pill.
15. How long does it _____ you to get to school?
16. If you want to _____ rich, you have to work hard.
17. I worked hard, but I didn't _____ much money.
18. That restaurant is usually crowded. You should _____ a reservation.
19. See you soon! _____ care of yourself!
20. I'm waiting for you to decide. _____ up your mind.
21. If you cook, I'll _____ the dishes.
22. I'm going to _____ a cake for her birthday.
23. Don't be sloppy. You should _____ your bed every morning.
24. He usually _____ to school at 9:00.
25. She's really friendly. She _____ along with everyone.

Supplies for a Deserted Island

There is a helicopter waiting on top of this building. It will take you to a deserted island far out in the Pacific Ocean (no people are there). You will be left there with your team. You have only a few minutes to decide what you are going to take with you. Your team can take only five items. Discuss which items you are going to take. You must all agree on only five items.

<u>*You cannot take cell phones, computers, or any items which will allow you to communicate. You will be completely isolated on this island.*</u>

AS YOU DISCUSS, REVIEW THE SENTENCE STRUCTURES YOU HAVE STUDIED:

Try to use GET, DO, MAKE, and TAKE.

We should take _____ .
If we take _____ , we will be able to make _____ .
We have to take _____ .
We must take _____ .
We don't have to take _____ .
_____ is more important than _____ .
_____ is the most useful item.
I have always used _____ for <u>(+ noun or verb+ing)</u>.
I have always used _____ to <u>(+ verb)</u> .

1. _____
2. _____
3. _____
4. _____
5. _____

9. Let's Talk about Experiences and Emotions

Photo by Pascal Reusch

This is a photograph of the view through the glass floor of the CN Tower in Toronto, Canada, which is 1,122 feet from the ground (342 meters). That is as far from the ground as the 112th floor of a building. When the tower was built in 1976, it was the tallest tower and the tallest free-standing building in the world. It is normal to feel frightened by heights, but an abnormal, irrational fear of heights is called acrophobia.

Photo by FEMA

Irrational fears are called phobias. A person who has a phobia understands there is no danger but is frightened anyway. It is normal to feel terrified when trapped under a building in an earthquake. As this photo of the January 17, 1994, Northridge earthquake shows, a collapsed building can be a frightening and dangerous place. An irrational fear of all small spaces, even everyday places such as elevators, is called claustrophobia.

A few spiders, such as the brown recluse on the left, are poisonous. We are lucky that the brown recluse does not live in California. Most spiders are harmless. Anyone who feels all spiders are horrifying, even if he or she knows the spiders are not poisonous, has what we would call arachnophobia.

People with phobias need help from professionals to overcome their fears. The rest of us can use our feelings to deal with many problems. If you feel

Photo by NASA

exhausted, it is time to rest. A confusing situation can inspire us to learn more or study harder. Even an embarrassing moment, although not so pleasant at the time, can seem quite funny weeks or years later and can provide us with a lot of good times and laughter.

ADJECTIVES ENDING IN "ED" | ADJECTIVES ENDING IN "ING"

THIS IS HOW SOMEONE FEELS	DESCRIBES A PERSON OR THING THAT MAKES OTHERS FEEL
bored	boring
confused	confusing
disappointed	disappointing
embarrassed	embarrassing
excited	exciting
exhausted	exhausting
frightened	frightening
horrified	horrifying
interested	interesting
shocked	shocking
surprised	surprising
terrified	terrifying
tired	tiring

Adjectives that end in "ED" describe how people or animals feel.

Adjectives that end in "ING" describe thINGS or people that are makING you or others feel.

Tell your partner about at least one of the subjects below. Describe in detail:

- the most **embarrassing** moment you have ever had. How embarrassed were you?
- the most **frightening** movie you have ever seen. Why was it so frightening? How frightened were you?
- the most **exciting** vacation. Where did you go? What did you do that was so exciting?
- the most **interesting** book you have ever read. When did you read it? How interested were you? Why were you so interested?
- the most **boring** experience you have ever had. Why were you so bored? Were other people as bored as you were?
- the most **terrifying** amusement park ride. Why were you so terrified? What were you afraid of?
- the most **confusing** experience you have ever had. Were others as confused as you were?
- the most **shocking** thing you have ever seen. Why were you so shocked?
- the most **tiring** day you have ever had. What made you so tired?
- the most **disappointing** experience you have ever had. Why were you so disappointed?

Now get ready to tell your story to the class!

10. Let's Talk without Mentioning Names

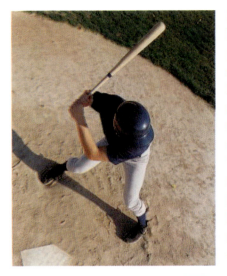

Kurt's parents always told him that he should play baseball in the park, but he and his brother liked to play in the backyard. One day when their parents were out, Kurt and his brother decided to practice. Kurt's brother pitched the ball, and Kurt swung the bat. After a few strikes, Kurt hit the ball. It flew right through the kitchen window! Glass was everywhere. They cleaned up the broken glass, but they were frightened. What would their parents do? For hours they sat on the back steps and discussed their options. They didn't have enough money to pay for a new window. They knew they couldn't tell a lie. In the end, they decided to tell the truth, but leave out exactly *who* broke the window. They used the passive voice.

- **Mother:** What happened?
- **Kurt:** The window was broken.

Active voice Passive voice

An expert will write the report. ⟶ The report will be written by an expert.

How to change the active to the passive:
1) **Put the object of the active sentence in place of the subject.**
   - The report
2) **Look at the tense of the verb.**
   - will write
3) **Put the verb "to be" in the tense of the verb in the active sentence.**
   - The report will be
4) **Put in the past participle form of the verb.**
   - The report will be written
5) **Optional: add "by" + the subject of the active sentence:**
   - The report will be written by an expert.

74

More examples:

Active ⟶ Passive

Bob broke the vase.   The vase was broken by Bob.
The mechanic should repair the car.   The car should be repaired by the mechanic.

An expert will set off the fireworks.   The fireworks will be set off by an expert.
The girls have eaten the cake.   The cake has been eaten by the girls.

CHANGE FROM THE ACTIVE VOICE TO THE PASSIVE VOICE:

1. Bob broke the window. _____
2. We will eat the cake. _____
3. Jane has written many notes. _____
4. The wind is blowing the tree against the house. _____
5. Jack usually feeds the dog. _____
6. The dentist canceled her appointment. _____
7. The mechanic should repair the car. _____
8. The secretary has called the clients. _____
9. He is going to set off the fireworks.. _____
10. The coach is going to postpone the game. _____
11. Jack painted that portrait. _____
12. The salesperson is helping me. _____
13. Their grandmother will take care of the children. _____
14. The person who made it should clean up the mess. _____
15. Steve Perlman invented a movie animation system called Contour. _____

Discuss with your partner:
What vegetables are grown in your country?
What animals are raised in your country?
What is made in your country?
What is manufactured in your country?
What was invented in your country?

GROWN / RAISED / MADE / MANUFACTURED / INVENTED

Where are (or were) things grown, raised, made, manufactured or invented?

Write down as many examples as you can. In a few minutes, your class will be divided into two teams.

You and your teammates will have to speak using passive sentences. Each team will get one point for one passive sentence. The team with the most points wins.

Example: *Paper was invented in China.*

REVIEW!

ANSWER IN COMPLETE SENTENCES: 1) What will you do if you win $1,000,000? 2) How do you drive? 3) Jack has a toothache. What should he do? 4) Have you ever arrived late to a movie? 5) What was invented in your country?	**ANSWER IN COMPLETE SENTENCES:** 1) What will you do if it is sunny next week? 2) How do you sing? 3) Linda is nervous. What should she do? 4) Have you ever seen a rattlesnake? 5) What fruits are grown in your country?
ANSWER IN COMPLETE SENTENCES: 1) What will you do if you find $100? 2) How do you sing? 3) Jane has a headache. What should she do? 4) Have you ever met anyone famous? 5) What vegetables are grown in your country?	**ANSWER IN COMPLETE SENTENCES:** 1) What will you do if it rains next weekend? 2) How do you dance? 3) John is tired. What should he do? 4) Have you ever seen a UFO? 5) What animals are raised in your country?
ANSWER IN COMPLETE SENTENCES: 1) What will you do if you get a flat tire? 2) How do you dance? 3) Bob has a backache. What should he do? 4) Have you ever dreamed in English? 5) What fruits are grown in your country?	**ANSWER IN COMPLETE SENTENCES:** 1) What will you do if it snows in Los Angeles? 2) How do you cook? 3) Jack's roommate is bad. What should he do? 4) Have you ever had a pet? 5) What was invented in your country?
ANSWER IN COMPLETE SENTENCES: 1) What will you do if you see a student cheating on a test? 2) How do you cook? 3) Mary is tired. What should she do? 4) Have you ever eaten pumpkin pie? 5) What is manufactured in your country?	**ANSWER IN COMPLETE SENTENCES:** 1) What will you do if you are hungry? 2) How do you drive? 3) Mary bought a dress she doesn't like. What should she do? 4) Have you ever stayed up all night? 5) What kind of food is made in your country?
ANSWER IN COMPLETE SENTENCES: 1) What will you do if you see a rat in your dormitory? 2) How do you swim? 3) Sally is lonely. What should she do? 4) Have you ever visited a country in Europe? 5) What kind of food is made in your country?	**ANSWER IN COMPLETE SENTENCES:** 1) What will you do if you can't find the key to your room? 2) How do you sing? 3) John has a backache. What should he do? 4) Have you ever visited a doctor in the U.S.? 5) What is manufactured in your country?
ANSWER IN COMPLETE SENTENCES: 1) What will you do if you see a cockroach in your kitchen? 2) How do you run? 3) Tom is bored. What should he do? 4) Have you ever lost your ID? 5) What flowers are grown in your country?	**ANSWER IN COMPLETE SENTENCES:** 1) What will you do if you see a rattlesnake? 2) How do you run? 3) John was bitten by a rattlesnake. What should he do? 4) Have you ever been bitten by a snake? 5) What animals are raised in your country?
ANSWER IN COMPLETE SENTENCES: 1) What will you do if you see a big dog? 2) How do you play chess? 3) Bob's room is dirty. What should he do? 4) Have you ever slept in class? 5) What animals are raised in your country?	**ANSWER IN COMPLETE SENTENCES:** 1) What will you do if you see a UFO? 2) How do you dance? 3) John is too thin. What should he do? 4) Have you ever been bitten by a dog? 5) What dogs are raised in your country?
ANSWER IN COMPLETE SENTENCES: 1) What will you do if you lose your homework? 2) How do you play tennis? 3) Alice has a sore throat. What should she do? 4) Have you ever gotten on the wrong bus? 5) Where was paper invented?	**ANSWER IN COMPLETE SENTENCES:** 1) What will you do if you see someone stealing a car? 2) How do you dance? 3) John has a toothache. What should he do? 4) Have you ever visited a dentist in the U.S.? 5) What flowers are grown in your country?

EXPLORATION

11. Getting around Town on Foot

Maria is at the corner of Sunset and Cahuenga Boulevards. She is lost and asks for help.

- **Maria:** Excuse me. **Do you know where Musso and Frank Grill is?**
- **John:** Of course. It's the oldest restaurant in Hollywood.
- **Maria: Can you tell me how to get there?**
- **John:** Are you driving or are you on foot?
- **Maria:** Well, I don't have a car.
- **John:** I hope you're wearing comfortable shoes. **Walk up** Cahuenga Boulevard to Hollywood Boulevard. **Cross** Hollywood Boulevard and **turn left**. **Keep walking along** Hollywood Boulevard. Musso and Frank Grill will be **on your right**.
- **Maria:** Thanks.
- **John:** There's a lot of history in that restaurant. Famous stars like Marilyn Monroe, Charlie Chaplin, and Elizabeth Taylor ate there a long time ago.
- **Maria:** Do you think I'll see anyone famous?
- **John:** If you do, don't act like a tourist. Stars don't want to be disturbed by people asking for autographs. If you want to see stars, find them on the Walk of Fame.
- **Maria:** Right. I'm planning to find Michael Jackson's star at 6927 Hollywood Boulevard. Do you know how I can find it?
- **John:** After you leave the restaurant, **walk west along** Hollywood Boulevard. His star is **on the corner of** Hollywood Boulevard and Highland Avenue.
- **Maria:** Is it on the north or the south side of Hollywood Boulevard?
- **John:** Always remember this: east is even, south the same. So 6927 is on the north side, the same as Musso and Frank and the Chinese Theatre, across from the Roosevelt Hotel.
- **Maria:** I don't understand. Could you explain that again?
- **John:** If the last number in an address is even, like 2, 4, 6, 8, it will be on the east or south side of a street. Odd numbers, like 1, 3 5, 7, are on the west or north side of a street. 6927 ends in 7, so it is on the north side of the street.
- **Maria:** Thank you so much. You have been **really** helpful.

PRACTICE ASKING FOR AND GIVING DIRECTIONS

Expressions to use and learn:
Excuse me. Can you tell me how to get to _____ from _____?
↑ Walk up _____. (usually a north/south street, or up a hill).
↓ Walk down _____. (usually a north/south street, or down a hill).
↔ Walk along _____ (an east/west street). ALSO: Walk east along _____. Walk west along _____.
⌐→ Turn right .   Turn left.   ←⌐ Cross the street.   _____ is across from _____.
ALSO: Keep (or continue) walking up/down/along _____.= Go straight up/down/along _____.

Practice with your partner. Ask for and give directions:
1. from the Roosevelt Hotel to Capitol Records.
2. from Capitol Records to Paramount Studios.
3. from Paramount Studios to the Cinerama Dome.
4. from the Cinerama Dome to the Chinese Theatre.
5. from the Chinese Theatre to the Crossroads of the World.

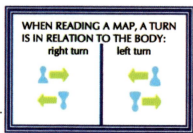

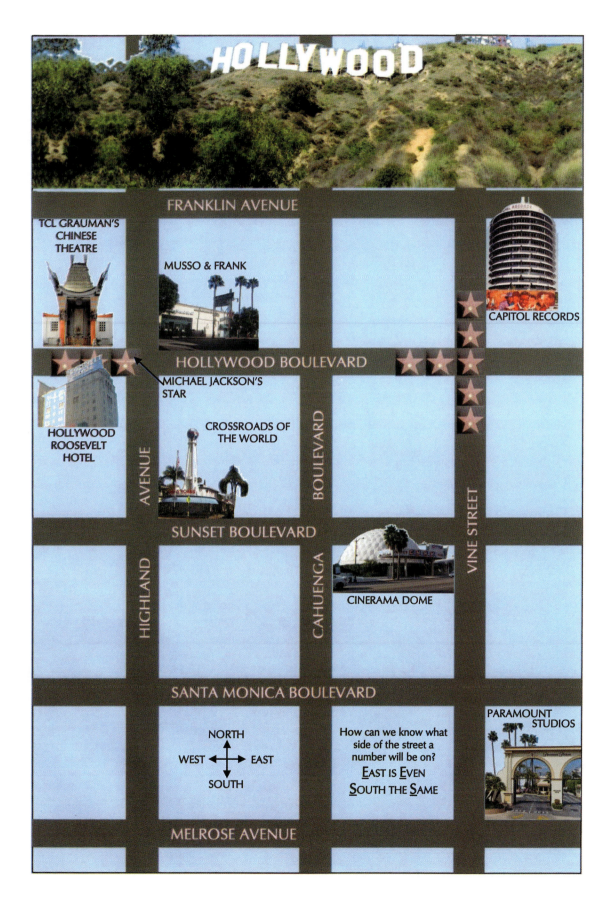

VOCABULARY: GETTING AROUND THE NEIGHBORHOOD

Below is a list of places. You will need to know these words to do the exercises on the following pages.

bakery = a shop which makes and sells bread, cakes, and cookies

beauty salon = a shop where people have their hair cut and styled, and where they have their nails polished, etc.

bookstore = a shop which sells books

café = a place where people can buy and drink coffee, tea, or eat snacks; also, a small restaurant.

copy shop = a place where people can make photocopies

dentist = a doctor who takes care of teeth

elementary school = a school for children who are twelve or younger

fitness center = a place where people can pay to use equipment to exercise

florist shop = a store which sells only flowers

gas station = a place where people buy gasoline for their cars and trucks

hardware store = a shop which sells tools

hospital = a place where sick people stay and where they are helped

ice cream shop = a place where people buy and eat only ice cream

laundromat = a public place where people can do their laundry by using money (coin-operated machines)

locksmith = a person who repairs and sells locks and keys, and opens locks

movie theater = a public place where people go to watch movies (films)

museum = a public place where people go to see art, history, or science shows (exhibitions)

pet shop = a store that sells pets (animals for the home) and supplies for pets

pharmacy = a store that sells medicine and drugs

post office = a government building where people can buy stamps, send letters and packages

shoe store = a shop which sells only shoes

supermarket = a big store that sells food

wine shop = a store that sells only wine

PRACTICE ASKING FOR AND GIVING DIRECTIONS
MAP FOR STUDENT A

Looking only at Map A, ask your partner:
Excuse me. Could you tell me how to get to

- the fitness center?
- the elementary school?
- the bookstore?
- the pharmacy?
- the laundromat?
- the copy shop?

- the bakery?
- the wine shop?
- the supermarket?
- the hardware store?
- the dentist?
- the café?

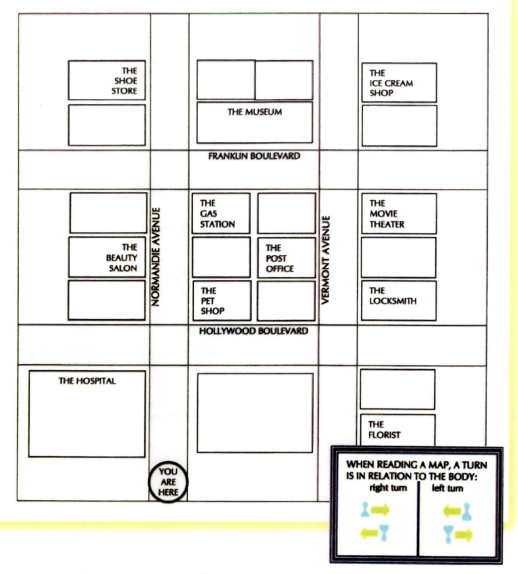

Practice again asking, "Can you tell me how to get to ____ from _____?"

Note: The maps on pages 81-82 are not real maps of Hollywood. The shops are not in these places.

PRACTICE ASKING FOR AND GIVING DIRECTIONS
MAP FOR STUDENT B

Looking only at Map B, ask your partner:
Excuse me. Could you tell me how to get to

- the shoe store?
- the ice cream shop?
- the locksmith?
- the beauty salon?
- the museum?
- the movie theater?
- the post office?
- the gas station?
- the hospital?
- the florist shop?
- Franklin Boulevard?
- the pet shop?

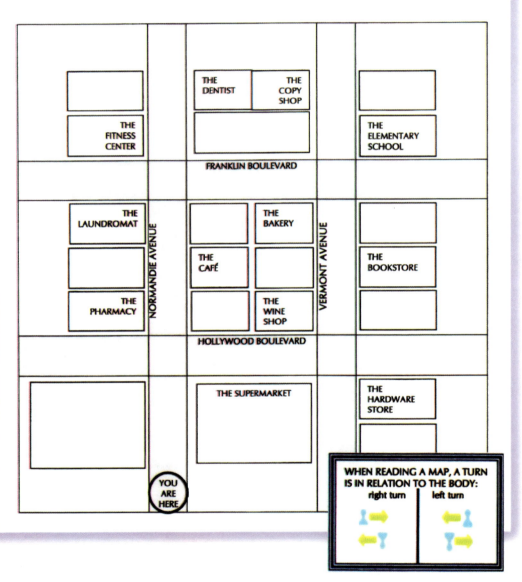

Practice again asking, "Can you tell me how to get to ____ from _____?"

Note: The maps on pages 81-82 are not real maps of Hollywood. The shops are not in these places.

Getting around Town by Bus

City Walk, Universal City

Bus schedules change. Don't rely on these times. Check metro.net.

- **David:** What are you doing this afternoon?
- **Kelly:** Nothing much. How about you?
- **David:** I'm going to Universal Studios.
- **Kelly:** Seriously? Do you have a car?
- **David:** No. I'm going by bus. It's easy. A bus leaves around every half hour.
- **Kelly:** Who told you that?
- **David:** No one. I checked out *Metro.net* and clicked on the *Metro Trip Planner* and got all the information I need. There's a bus called Universal Studios on Lassen Street and Reseda Boulevard.
- **Kelly:** Do you mean the bus has a name?
- **David:** It's the head sign. You know, the sign on the front of the bus. It goes to Universal Studios.
- **Kelly:** Is it expensive?
- **David:** No, it isn't. And a metro.net app for your phone is free.
- **Kelly:** It must be a long trip.
- **David:** About an hour and a half. But if you're with someone, time flies. Do you want to come?
- **Kelly:** Sure. Where should I meet you?
- **David:** On the northwest corner of Reseda and Lassen. The bus leaves at 2:20. Don't be late! If we leave by 2:20, we'll be there by 3:43. That will give us plenty of time to explore. But we have to be careful. The last Reseda/Devonshire bus leaves Universal City Station/Bus Bay 1 at 12:34 AM. We can't miss that!
- **Kelly:** 12:34 AM? I don't want to stay out that late.
- **David:** No worries. We'll come home earlier.

Check *Metro.net* to learn how to get to places such as TCL Grauman's Chinese Theatre, the Getty Museum, Griffith Park, Olvera Street, and La Brea Tar Pits.

12. Prehistoric California: La Brea Tar Pits

Match the pictures of the prehistoric animals with their names.

1. ____ EAGLE

2. ____ SHORT-FACED BEAR

3. ____ MAMMOTH

4. ____ COYOTE

5. ____ SABER-TOOTHED CAT

6. ____ CAMEL

7. ____ WESTERN HORSE

8. ____ GIANT SLOTH

9. ____ BISON

10. ____ DIRE WOLF

A.

B.

C.

D.

E.

F.

G.

H.

I.

J.

**Page Museum, 5801 Wilshire Boulevard, Los Angeles, CA, 90036
Open 9:30 A.M. – 5:00 P.M. Every Day / Telephone (323) 857-6300 ex. 110**
(CHECK FOR UPDATES)

If you want to know what Southern California was like in **prehistoric** times before **human settlement**, you are lucky. Nowhere else in the world is there such a large collection of Ice Age **fossils**. At the end of the Pleistocene **Epoch**, about 40,000 years ago, plants and animals were trapped in asphalt **pits** in the area that is now Los Angeles. Dinosaurs lived 65 million years before that. Although called **tar** pits, the pits contain asphalt, not tar. Tar is made **commercially**, and **asphalt** occurs naturally. In Spanish, "brea" means tar.

This area used to be under the Pacific Ocean. When marine plants and animals died, their **remains** fell to the bottom of the ocean and the asphalt was created after millions of years of aging. This is also how **fossil fuels**, such as petroleum, were formed.

Later, when the ocean **receded**, the land around Los Angeles was no longer covered by water. Asphalt bubbled up and slowly came to the **surface** and made pools. Asphalt is very sticky. When animals fell into the pools, they could not get out. They were **trapped.** They died and their bones were **preserved** very well under the asphalt. Their bones became **fossils**.

Researchers are digging up the fossils and learning a lot about what this area was like long ago. Frogs used to live here. That means there were streams and the climate was humid, not as dry as it is today. Although it was in the Ice Age, there was no permanent ice here. The climate was not much colder than it is today. If you take a trip to San Francisco, you will know what the climate of Los Angeles was like during the Ice Age.

Some of the **extinct** animals found in the La Brea pits include bison, mammoths, ground sloths, short-faced bears, and a wolf that is different from the modern wolf. Also found in the pits were saber-toothed cats, sometimes mistakenly called tigers. People are so fascinated by them that the saber-toothed cat became the official state fossil of California.

A saber is a curved sword, or very long knife, and these cats had long curved teeth. By examining the fossils, researchers can even understand how these cats lived. Some were found with **healed** bones. An animal with broken bones cannot hunt. This means that these cats were taken care of and fed by other cats until their bones healed. They probably lived in a social group, or pride, like modern-day lions.

The largest bird found in the asphalt was Merriam's Teratorn. Unlike the modern-day condor, which is a **scavenger**, it killed its food. It hunted by walking on the ground, not by flying like an eagle. Its wingspan was ten feet (over three meters) and it weighed thirty pounds (over thirteen kilograms).

Imagine finding all these fossils in the center of a city! If you get a chance to visit the Page Museum La Brea Tar Pits, you are in for a real treat. You will learn about many plants and animals. You will see many fossil skeletons, and you will even get to pull a metal bar out of asphalt so that you can feel how difficult it was and is to get out of the pits. Animals continue to get trapped there.

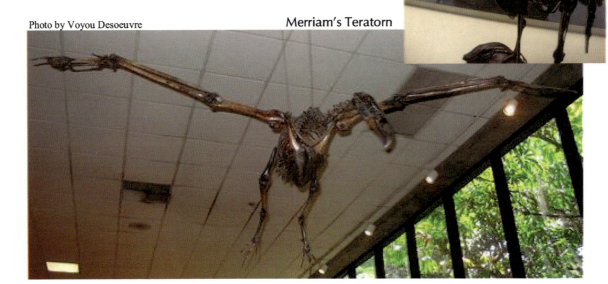

Photo by Voyou Desoeuvre — Merriam's Teratorn

VOCABULARY: MATCHING - MATCH WITHIN THE SAME COLOR

1. ____prehistoric
2. ____human
3. ____settlement
4. ____pit
5. ____epoch

A. a person
B. of the time before people wrote things
C. a hole in the ground
D. a long period of time
E. a place where people begin to live

6. ____commercially
7. ____asphalt
8. ____tar
9. ____marine
10. ____remains

F. a black substance made in a commercial process
G. concerning the ocean
H. what is left
I. a sticky, naturally occurring, black substance
J. for business

11. ____fossil
12. ____fossil fuel
13. ____to recede
14. ____surface
15. ____trapped

K. the top of something
L. to move away from
M. preserved plants/animals from millions of years ago
N. not able to leave
O. something burned for energy that was made from dead plants and animals, dead for millions of years

16. ____to preserve
17. ____extinct
18. ____to heal
19. ____scavenger
20. ____span

P. to return to health
Q. the distance from one end to the other
R. to keep something from changing
S. not existing anymore; not alive anymore
T. a person/animal that eats/uses garbage or dead things

True or False

1. ____ Dinosaurs were trapped in the asphalt.
2. ____ Scientists know that Los Angeles used to be more humid.
3. ____ Tar is not the same as asphalt.
4. ____ Saber-toothed cats probably hunted alone.
5. ____ The largest bird found in the pits was a scavenger.

DISCUSSION AND CRITICAL THINKING

1. California condors, burrowing owls, Taiwanese pink dolphins, pandas, polar bears, and other animals are endangered, which means they might soon become extinct.
Is it important to keep these animals from extinction?
What can scientists learn from these animals?
Can scientists learn anything to help humans?
2. Why do some people think we have to stop using fossil fuels? What do you think?

Speaking about Habits in the Past

USED TO + VERB
I **used to study** English in Korea.

Note on pronunciation:

I **use** Skype to speak to my parents in Korea. The "s" in "**use**" has vibrations (put your hand on your throat and feel them). This voiced "s" sounds like a "z."

I **used to** call them by phone. The "t" in "to" has no vibrations (put your hand on your throat; you feel nothing). It goes with a voiceless "s" in "**used to**" that has no vibrations. The "ed" is not pronounced. It sounds like "use to."

Don't let the pronunciation confuse you!

Did you **use** to e-mail them?   **SAME FORM AS:**   **Did** you **live** in Seoul?
No, I **used** to telephone them.   No, I **lived** in Busan.

- **David:** Where are you from?
- **Kelly:** Korea.
- **David:** Really? You speak English well. Where did you study?
- **Kelly:** Actually, I'm still studying English at school.
- **David:** Are you serious? How long have you been studying?
- **Kelly:** I've been here only a few weeks, but I **used to study** in Korea. I was pretty focused and I **used to study** hard.
- **David:** Did you do anything besides studying?
- **Kelly:** Sure. I **used to go dancing** every Saturday, and whenever I got the chance I **used to go hiking** outside the city.

Practice in Pairs Using "Used to"

Ask your partner:
1. What did you use to do when you were in your country? **Answer:** I used to (verb)….
2. What did you use to eat when you were in your country? **Answer:** I used to (verb)….
3. What did you use to do in your free time in your country? **Answer:** I used to (verb)….
4. Where did you use to go on vacation in your country? **Answer:** I used to (verb)….
5. What did you use to like to do when you were little? **Answer:** I used to (verb)….

SPECIAL EXPRESSIONS: GO VERB+ING

go swimming	go camping
go shopping	go hiking
go dancing	go fishing
go skating	go hunting
go skiing	go sailing
go bowling	go surfing
go jogging	go skydiving
go running	go rollerblading

DON'T FORGET: NO "ED" IN THE QUESTION, "WHAT DID YOU USE TO DO?"

Practice asking your partner. Try to speak non-stop for five minutes. Start with these questions:

What did you use to do on weekends in your country?
What did you use to do for vacation?
What did you use to do in the evenings?

Human Bingo

Find someone who used to do these activities.
Ask your classmates questions: **Did you use to go ----ing in your country?**
Cross off a square when you find someone who used to do that activity. When you have crossed off enough squares to make a vertical, horizontal, or diagonal line, say BINGO!

go camping	go swimming in the ocean	go dancing in nightclubs	go swimming in a pool
go skydiving	go bowling	go jogging in the morning	go skateboarding
go fishing in a river	go skiing in the mountains	go shopping at a farmers' market	go hiking
go rollerblading	go surfing	go sailing	go ice skating

13. The First People
The Gabrielinos, Tataviam, and Chumash

When Columbus landed in America, he met people he thought were Indians. They were not Indians, although today we sometimes still call them American Indians. It is more accurate to call them Native Americans, or simply the First People.

A Tongva Woman, Mrs. James V. Rosemeyre, 1905.

The First People who lived in the area around Los Angeles, the Tataviam, Gabrielinos, and Chumash, were all peaceful. There was very little crime in their communities, and when the Spanish came, they did not fight.

In 1542, the Spanish explorer Juan Rodriguez Cabrillo arrived at Santa Catalina Island. The people who met him were known by many names, but later were often called Gabrielinos because they lived near the **Mission** San Gabriel Arcángel, which was built in 1771. At that time, they had a population of about 5,000. A Gabrielino village called Yaanga was in the place of our present Civic Center of Los Angeles.

In 1797, Mission San Fernando Rey de España was **founded**. This is in Mission Hills in the San Fernando Valley. The Tataviam lived in this area, and were often known as Fernandeños because they lived near that mission. There were only around 1,000 of them. Now the descendents of the Gabrielinos and Fernandeños are known as Tongva.

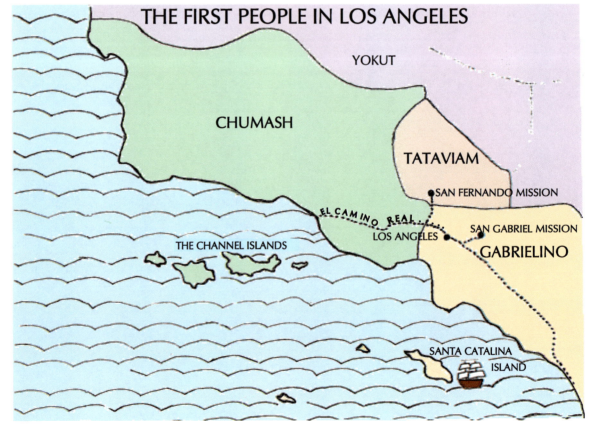

90

By far the largest group of Native Americans, the Chumash, lived in the coastal areas north of the Gabrielinos. At the time of the Spanish arrival, there were 22,000. The groups of Chumash who lived on the Channel Islands made money from **shells**, and the name Chumash means the shell **bead** money makers. After a while, this name was used for all the related groups that lived in the area. They were expert fishermen, and made excellent boats sealed with pine pitch and **asphalt**. These boats, called "tomol," were often made from **redwood** which drifted up on the shore.

A Chumash Boat, Tomol, near the Channel Islands

An Ap, or Chumash House, at the Chumash Museum in Thousand Oaks

The Chumash houses ("ap") were round and **thatched**, made from sticks and plants. The most important Chumash food was made from **acorns**.

We still use the Chumash language every day for names of places. Some cities, such as Malibu, have Chumash names. "Malibu" means "the surf makes a loud sound" (the ocean makes a loud noise).

THE CHUMASH WERE ALSO GREAT BASKET WEAVERS.

The Chumash lived by three **principles**: **limitation**, **moderation**, and **compensation**. This **philosophy** required each person to **recognize** his or her limits and abilities as a unique individual, although equal to all others in the society. Moderation was important to keep in balance with nature when using **resources** from the land and the ocean. They used the principle of moderation in their work. They believed that **haste** makes waste, so they worked carefully even if it took more time. The Chumash valued giving without expecting **tangible** compensation because they understood that payment for kindness is not always monetary or **material**.

This thoughtful way of life was not understood by the Spanish or Americans, who lived (and still live) for **profit**. When they joined the missions, the Chumash, Gabrielinos, and Tataviam were forced to give up their culture. When Mexico gained its independence from Spain in 1821, many of the Native Americans were **enslaved** by Mexicans. They also **suffered** two **smallpox epidemics**, one in 1840 and another in 1860, which were caused by contact with this new disease brought by the European **settlers**.

In 1848, California became part of United States territory, and it became the 31st state in 1850. As Americans moved in to **claim** land, the Native Americans **suffered** even more. A writer who was interested in the problems facing the Native Americans was Helen Hunt Jackson. Although she had previously published *A Century of **Dishonor***, which was a record of how the U.S. government had cheated various Native American tribes, she was **disappointed** that her book did not change public opinion. Knowing that the **novel** *Uncle Tom's Cabin* by Harriet Beecher Stowe, which was published in 1852, was so important in forming public opinion that it contributed to the start of the Civil War and the freeing of the African-American **slaves** in 1863, Ms. Jackson decided to write a novel. In 1883 she wrote *Ramona*, the story of a rich Mexican girl who fell in love with a Tataviam worker on her family's ranch. The novel was a huge hit and created a focus for the tourist industry in California which lasted into the 1960s. Sadly, the book did not bring attention to the problems of the First People.

Although we will never know for sure the exact ranch that Ms. Jackson wrote about in *Ramona*, many think that Rancho Camulos was the place where this **fictional romance** took place. You may visit Rancho Camulos in Piru, and you may read the entire novel *Ramona* on the ranch website.

An Ap, or Chumash House, Partially Built in the Satwiwa Natural Area

By 1900, most of the First People of Southern California had died. Their culture had been almost completely destroyed. Now 300 people claim Gabrielino (Tongva) **heritage**, and there are about 2,000 Chumash. You may visit the Chumash Museum in Thousand Oaks or the Chumash Discovery Village at Nicholas Canyon County Beach Park in Malibu. In both places you may see new copies of the original Chumash houses.

When California became a state, the U.S. government pushed the First People onto **reservations**, land which was often so bad that it was difficult to make a living there. In the 1980s, new laws made it possible for Native Americans to start gaming businesses on their reservations. They finally began to make more money.

Games have always been a part of Native American culture. The Chumash played sports and many other games. They also gambled, or played games for money. Today, their new gaming businesses, or casinos, make enough money for many groups to return to a good life and be self-sufficient. As always, the Chumash think giving is important. They have given millions of dollars to organizations and people in need.

Like casinos in Las Vegas, Native American casinos offer music, entertainment, bingo, and games. In Southern California, you may visit the Chumash Casino Resort in Santa Barbara County; the San Manuel Indian Bingo and Casino, owned by the San Manuel Band of Serrano Mission Indians in San Bernardino County; or the largest casino, Pechanga Resort and Casino, in Riverside County, which is owned by one of the six bands of the Luiseño people who lived near the Mission San Luis Rey de Francía, founded in 1798.

VOCABULARY: MATCHING - MATCH WITHIN THE SAME COLOR

Set #1
1. _____ to found
2. _____ a string of beads
3. _____ shell
4. _____ asphalt
5. _____ acorn
6. _____ redwood
7. _____ thatched
8. _____ basket
9. _____ to weave
10. _____ principle
11. _____ limitation
12. _____ moderation
13. _____ compensation
14. _____ philosophy
15. _____ to recognize
16. _____ resource
17. _____ haste
18. _____ tangible

A. ⟶
B. ⟶
C. ⟶
D. to start a town, business, or organization
E. an enormous tree with reddish wood
F. a sticky, naturally occurring, black substance
G. the end of what is possible; the best one can do
H. covered with dried straw or plants (usually a roof)
I. a container made of woven plants
J. to connect fibers or plants together, over and under
K. balance, without extremes
L. an idea or rule about what is right or wrong
M. a natural item that is used
N. to accept and understand; also, realize you know
O. hurry
P. able to be touched
Q. payment for something given, done, or suffered
R. the study of knowledge, life, and what is good or bad

Set #2
1. _____ material
2. _____ profit
3. _____ to enslave
4. _____ smallpox
5. _____ epidemic
6. _____ settler
7. _____ to claim
8. _____ mission
9. _____ to suffer
10. _____ dishonor
11. _____ disappointed
12. _____ novel
13. _____ slave
14. _____ fiction
15. _____ romance
16. _____ heritage
17. _____ reservation
18. _____ illegal

A. a serious, often deadly disease that leaves scars
B. a person who begins to live in a place
C. extra money you earn that is beyond expenses
D. something that spreads quickly among many people
E. of money or things rather than mind or spirit
F. to force to work without payment or ability to leave
G. a long fiction book (not a true story)
H. unhappy because you expected something better
I. lack of respect because you have done wrong
J. a building for people who spread their religion
K. to have pain, a bad experience, or an illness
L. to say you own something or have a right to it
M. against the law
N. a wonderful love experience or story
O. a person owned by another and forced to work
P. an area of land for Native Americans
Q. a story, usually for entertainment, that is not true
R. the traditions of a group

READING COMPREHENSION

1. Who was the first Spanish explorer to visit the Los Angeles area?

2. When did he arrive? Where did he arrive?

3. Did the Native Americans welcome him or fight him?

4. Which Native Americans lived in Los Angeles?

5. Which Native Americans lived in the San Fernando Valley?

6. Which Native Americans lived in Malibu?

7. What did the Chumash use as money?

8. What does the word "Chumash" mean?

9. What did the Chumash use to make their boats? Name three things:

10. What was their most important food?

11. What are the three principles that the Chumash lived by?

12. Why did so many Native Americans die in the 1800s?

13. When did California become part of United States territory?

14. When did California become the 31st state?

15. Why did Helen Hunt Jackson write a novel?

16. What was the name of Helen Hunt Jackson's novel? What was it about?

17. Did Helen Hunt Jackson's novel bring attention to the problems of Native Americans?

18. How do many Native Americans make a living today?

DISCUSSION AND CRITICAL THINKING

1. Talk about the Chumash philosophy. How can people be different and equal?
2. What principles do you live your life by? Do you live for profit? Why or why not?
3. Has living for profit created any problems in our society? Explain.
4. What principles do you recommend for society? Why?

CRITICAL THINKING: WHAT DO YOU HAVE TO HAVE? WHAT DON'T YOU HAVE TO HAVE?

Consider the comments the Native Americans made about their lifestyle. Think about creating a new society. What would you want to take with you into this new world? What wouldn't you want to take? The following pictures might give you some ideas. What is really necessary to live a good life? Jot down a few notes. **Discuss.**

What do you have to have?	**What don't you have to have?**
_____	_____
_____	_____
_____	_____
_____	_____
_____	_____

The Iroquois League and the U.S. Federal System

If you plan on visiting another state, it is important to know that each state has different laws. Some laws may change from state to state, such as whether you can smoke in restaurants, bars, or public places. In California, people cannot smoke in bars or restaurants. Cities may have additional laws, such as whether people can smoke in parks. Each state **retains** independence in such cases even as it is part of the union. The United States **federal** government is like an umbrella unifying all the states for all major laws. The states of the union are all under this umbrella.

When the U.S. Constitution was written in 1787 (**approved** in 1788 and in use since 1789), there were no living European examples of a democratic federal system.

Each of the thirteen colonies had its own **customs** and in some cases did not agree with laws in other states. For example, there was **slavery** in the southern states but not in the northern states. On the other hand, the early Americans of all states wanted to come together to help each other in their common interests. Not many people understand how our **founding** fathers came up with the idea for a federal system.

A Native American, the Iroquois Chief Canassatego, recommended this system to the British in 1744, forty-three years before the U.S. Constitution was written. He told the British that it was difficult for the Iroquois to talk to and deal with the **colonies** because they did not have a **unified policy**. He recommended a **constitution** similar to his, the *Kaianerekowa* (Great Law of Peace) of the Iroquois **League**.

The *Kaianerekowa* was **established** sometime before 1600 by two Native American men named Dekanewidah and Hiawatha. The Iroquois League extended from Pennsylvania to Ohio and from Canada to Kentucky. It was made up of six nations: the Onondaga, Cayuga, Mohawk, Oneida, Seneca, and Tuscarora. The women of each nation voted to elect men representatives who were called *sachems* to form a council to decide policies for each nation. Furthermore, the *sachems* met to agree upon laws and actions for the entire league. They had careful **procedures** and checks and balances between the nations. The Ononadaga, as "Fire Keepers," had final **approval**. If they did not agree, they had **veto** power and the approval **process** started all over again until the nations reached a **unanimous** decision.

In the 1750s, Benjamin Franklin worked as Indian **commissioner** for the colony of Pennsylvania. He studied the Iroquois customs and their government and was in a position to recommend the **adoption** of their system. In 1754 he recommended that the colonies form a union similar to that of the Iroquois, but that didn't happen until the U.S. Constitution was written. Our two houses of Congress, the Senate and the House of Representatives, **mirror** the decision-making process of the nations of the Iroquois League, and the veto power of the U.S. President is similar to that of the "Fire Keepers," the Onondaga Nation.

VOCABULARY: MATCHING - MATCH WITHIN THE SAME COLOR

Set #1

1. _____ to retain
2. _____ federal
3. _____ to approve
4. _____ custom
5. _____ slavery
6. _____ founding
7. _____ colony
8. _____ unified
9. _____ policy
10. _____ constitution

A. a system of owning people to force them to work
B. a tradition
C. of the central government of a country with states
D. to formally agree to something
E. to keep
F. combined into one
G. written laws that govern a country
H. describing a person who starts something
I. an area ruled by a country that is far away
J. an official rule or way of doing things

Set #2

1. _____ league
2. _____ to establish
3. _____ procedure
4. _____ approval
5. _____ veto
6. _____ process
7. _____ unanimous
8. _____ commissioner
9. _____ adoption
10. _____ to mirror

A. a way of doing something
B. a group joined together with similar interests
C. an official agreement or acceptance
D. to disagree and not allow a law to be created
E. to start a business, country, etc.
F. a person hired by an official group
G. a decision to have or use something as one's own
H. a system of actions to get a particular result
I. to be similar
J. when everyone agrees

DISCUSSION AND CRITICAL THINKING

1. Can you think of laws that are different from one country to another or from one state to another?
2. What laws do you think you should know before going into another state or country?
3. How are laws made in your country?
4. When did women get the right to vote in your country? Why do you think it took so long?
5. Do you think the Iroquois were very advanced in their way of thinking? Were you surprised to learn of the league of the Iroquois? Why or why not?
6. Why did the Iroquois call their system of government the Great Law of Peace?
7. Can you think of a system which would bring peace to the whole world?
8. What changes have to be made in the world before that can happen?
9. Why do you think the Iroquois succeeded in having hundreds of years of peace when we cannot have peace?
10. Do you think we will ever have world peace?

14. El Camino Real

El Camino Real (the Royal Road) follows the coast of California. It connects the 21 missions built by the Spanish from 1769 to 1823. In the beginning, it was just a path. **It took a day** by horseback to get from one mission to another, a distance of 30 miles (or 48 kilometers). It curves inland to go to the missions in the area of Los Angeles: the San Fernando Mission and the San Gabriel Mission. This road has been used continuously up to the present day: Our freeways have been built along this trail!

In Los Angeles, the 101 freeway and the 5 freeway to San Diego follow the old road. People say that missionaries threw mustard seeds along the road so travelers would not lose their way. In the spring and early summer, you can still see the yellow flowers blooming along the 101 freeway. Although beautiful, these plants are not native.

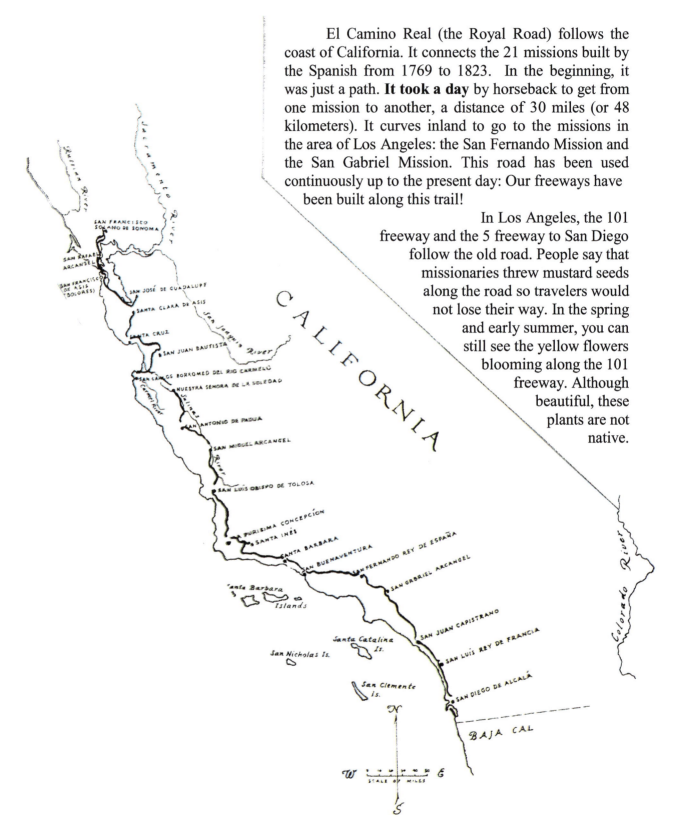

At the time the modern highway was built, it was not common to have road signs. In order to commemorate the historic trail, 450 bells manufactured by the California Bell Company were placed along the road. The first bell was put up in 1906. Over the years, the bells have been repaired and replaced. In 2005, 555 new bells were manufactured by the same company and placed along the route. You can see a bell every one or two miles. Have you seen these bells?

How California Got Its Name

At the time California was discovered, a popular novel written by Garci Rodríguez de Montalvo described a beautiful island which was called California. The explorers saw Baja California and thought it was an island. They named it after the fabulous island in the story.

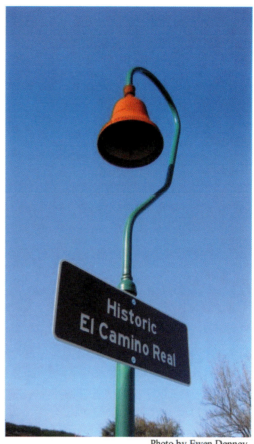
Photo by Ewen Denney

Practice:
It Takes Time

It used to take one day by horse to travel from one mission to another. How long do you think it would take you by car?

How long does it take you to   It takes (me) . . . .
- get to school?
- get to the supermarket?
- make dinner?
- make breakfast?
- clean the bathroom?

How long did it take you to   It took (me) . . . .
- fly from your country?
- get a passport and a visa?
- learn how to drive / ride a bicycle?
- learn how to use a cell phone?
- learn how to type on the computer?

How long does it take to   It takes . . . .
- drive to Las Vegas?
- get to Universal Studios by bus?

15. El Pueblo de Los Angeles Historical Monument, Olvera Street, and Avila Adobe, the Oldest House in Los Angeles

Avila Adobe, Olvera Street

El Pueblo de Los Angeles Historical Monument
125 Paseo de la Plaza

On August 2, 1769, Father Crespi and his group of **explorers** gave a long name to a beautiful river in Southern California. Father Crespi was a Franciscan, a member of a Catholic religious group **founded** by Saint Francis of Assisi. On the Franciscan calendar, August 2 was a special feast day at a small chapel used by St. Francis of Assisi in Italy. The chapel is on a small piece, or portion, of land ("porziuncola"). In the chapel is a fresco, a wall painting, of St. Mary surrounded by **angels**. This chapel became known as "Saint Mary of the Angels on the Small Portion." In honor of this feast day at the chapel, Father Crespi gave the river a name in Spanish, "Río de Nuestra Señora la Reina de los Angeles de Porciúncula" (River of Our Lady the Queen of the Angels of the Small Portion).

The Tongva village, Yaanga, was near the river. On September 4, 1781, when California was part of the Spanish Empire, a group of eleven families, including forty-four men, women, and children, came from what is now northwestern Mexico to **found** a new town for Spain near Yaanga. Only two of the settlers were actually from Spain. The others, like most people in northwestern Mexico at that time, were from mixed **ethnic** groups: Native American, African, and European. These **settlers** named their new town "El Pueblo de Nuestra Señora la Reina de los Angeles del Río de Porciúncula." Now we call it Los Angeles.

In 1810, Francisco Avila was **mayor** of Los Angeles. In about 1818, he built a house, Avila Adobe, which is now the oldest house still **standing** in LA. An adobe is made from sun-dried clay, or earth. The Avila Adobe is **furnished** and open to the **public** so that **visitors** can get an idea of what it was like to live in the 1800s.

Photo by Brenard Gagnon

Avila Adobe Kitchen

Los Angeles has always been a place of **ethic diversity**. In the 1820s, Italians began to arrive. Many, like Antonio Pelanconi, started **wineries**. Los Angeles became the center of the Californian **wine industry**. A restaurant is now in the Pelanconi house on Olvera Street, the oldest **brick** building still standing in Los Angeles. His winery was in a building across the street. In fact, Olvera Street was once known as **Vine** Street because of all the wineries that were there in the past.

Soon after the Italians, the French came. Starting in the 1850s, many Chinese came and made important **contributions** to the city as **entrepreneurs**, **professionals**, and **agricultural producers**.

Pío Pico, the Last Mexican Governor of California, and the Pico House, Which He Built in 1869-1870

Afro-Mexicans were important from the first Spanish **settlement**. Twenty-six of the **original** forty-four settlers were Afro-Mexicans. The most famous Afro-Mexican in the history of California was Pío Pico. He was born in 1801 at Mission San Gabriel and was the last Mexican governor from 1845-1846. You can visit his house near Olvera Street.

After Mexico gained its **independence** from Spain in 1821, Los Angeles was part of Mexico. Then, with the Guadalupe Hidalgo Treaty which ended the Mexican-American War in 1848, California became part of the United States (although it was an independent **republic** for six months from 1846-1847). In 1850, California became the 31st state of the United States.

In the 1850s, several **former slaves** arrived from the southern United States. One woman, Bridget "Biddy" Mason, was taken to Los Angeles as a slave and won her **freedom** in court because **slavery** was **illegal** in California. She spoke Spanish and English, became an important businesswoman and **land owner**, and sometimes ate dinner at the Pico House. You can learn more about her at the Biddy Mason Park from 3rd Street to 4th Street between Spring Street and Broadway.

Many **minority ethnic** groups have lived in Los Angeles and have made it the **cosmopolitan** city that it is today. Now most people in Los Angeles are Mexican Americans.

La Placita Church, Main Street

ON THE FRONT OF LA PLACITA CHURCH
A MOSAIC REPRODUCTION OF A DETAIL OF THE PAINTING IN ASSISI
THAT INSPIRED THE NAMING OF LOS ANGELES

VOCABULARY: MATCHING - MATCH WITHIN THE SAME COLOR

1. ____ explorer
2. ____ to furnish
3. ____ public
4. ____ to found
5. ____ settler
6. ____ angel
7. ____ mayor
8. ____ ethnic
9. ____ diversity
10. ____ winery
11. ____ wine
12. ____ brick
13. ____ vine
14. ____ contribution
15. ____ entrepreneur

A. all people
B. a person who begins to live in a place
C. to put furniture (chairs, tables, etc.) in a place
D. to start a town or a company
E. a person who travels in and studies unknown areas
F. noun: having many different kinds
G. a spirit who helps God
H. a place where wine is made
I. the leader of a city
J. of people with a particular culture
K. a plant that climbs; often a grape plant
L. someone who starts a business
M. a very hard block of clay used for building
N. alcoholic, fermented juice of grapes or fruit
O. something given along with others who give

Set #2

1. ____ professional
2. ____ agricultural
3. ____ producer
4. ____ settlement
5. ____ original
6. ____ independence
7. ____ republic
8. ____ former
9. ____ slave
10. ____ freedom
11. ____ slavery
12. ____ illegal
13. ____ land
14. ____ owner
15. ____ minority
16. ____ cosmopolitan

A. of farming, or growing food
B. noun: not being controlled by others
C. a place where people begin to live
D. a person who makes or grows things
E. a person who gets a job after study (doctor, etc.)
F. the first
G. a system of owning people to force them to work
H. a country which elects its leaders
I. noun: being free, not owned by anyone
J. a person owned by another and forced to work
K. in the past
L. having all parts of the world in it
M. someone who has something
N. a small part
O. against the law
P. earth, soil, to build on, or grow plants on

READING COMPREHENSION

1. What is the oldest house in Los Angeles? Where is it? When was it built?
2. Who lived in the area of Los Angeles before the settlers for the Spanish Empire?
3. Where did the first settlers for the Spanish Empire come from?
4. How many were there?
5. How many were Spanish? What ethnic groups were the other first settlers from?
6. What other ethnic groups came later?
7. Who was Pío Pico?
8. When did California become a state of the United States?
9. Who was Biddy Mason? Where can you learn more about her?
10. What is the largest ethnic group in Los Angeles today?

DISCUSSION AND CRITICAL THINKING

1. At times in the past, there were problems between the many ethnic groups in Los Angeles. Have you heard of problems between ethnic groups in your country or in other countries?
2. Why do you think there are or were problems?
3. What can we do to end these problems?

Looking for Souvenirs

- **Maria:** Olvera Street is a great place to buy **souvenirs**. There are some interesting **candle** shops here.
- **Yevgenia:** Candles? I'd like to buy a **purse**.
- **Maria:** Purses are so expensive.
  Yevgenia talks to the salesclerk:
- **Yevgenia:** Excuse me. How much does this **purse** cost?
- **Salesclerk:** Twenty-five dollars.
- **Yevgenia:** Is it **leather**?
- **Salesclerk:** Yes, it is.
- **Yevgenia:** I'd like to buy it, please.
- **Maria:** I don't think it's **leather.**
- **Yevgenia:** Smell it.
- **Maria:** You're right. It's leather! This is a **bargain**.

Vocabulary: Match the Word with the Definition on the Right

1. _____ a souvenir
2. _____ candle
3. _____ a purse
4. _____ a salesclerk
5. _____ leather
6. _____ a bargain

A. animal skin (no fur/hair) used to make things
B. wax stick burned for light
C. someone who sells in a store or shop
D. something good for a low price
E. something to keep to remember
F. a bag that women use to carry things

DISCUSSION AND CRITICAL THINKING

1. Yevgenia smelled the purse to make sure it was leather. Do you think smelling the purse is a good way to make sure it is leather?
2. What are good ways to make sure you will be happy with what you buy?

Practice Asking for Prices

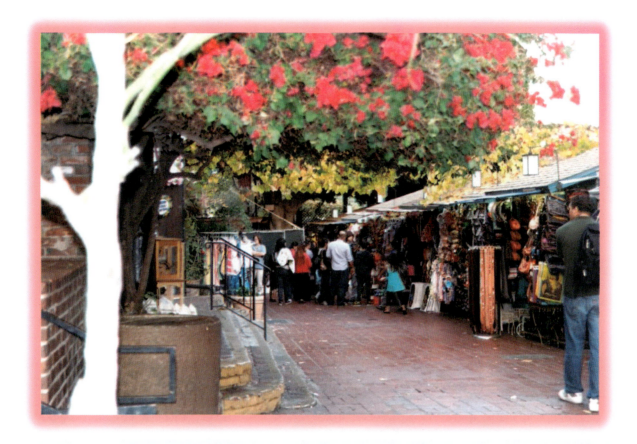

Ask for the cost of one item (singular):
Maria: How much **does** the dress cost?
Salesclerk: It **costs** $40.
Maria: How much **does** the meat cost?
Salesclerk: It **costs** $3 a pound.
(or: It costs $3 per pound.)

Ask for the cost of two items (plural):
Maria: How much **do** the sandals cost?
Salesclerk: They **cost** $20.
Maria: How much **do** the oranges cost?
Salesclerk: They **cost** $2 a pound.
(or: They cost $2 per pound.)

Role play with your partner. One of you is the salesclerk and one of you is the customer. Then change roles.

Ask for the cost of one item (singular):
1. the blouse
2. the shirt
3. the book
4. the doll
5. the toy, etc.

Ask for the cost of two items (plural):
1. the pants
2. the jeans
3. the cookies
4. the doughnuts
5. the shoes, etc.

16. The San Fernando Mission

15151 San Fernando Mission Boulevard, CA 91345-1109
Open Daily from 9 A.M. to 4:30 P.M./ Telephone: (818) 361-0186 (CHECK FOR UPDATES)

In what was once called the Valley of Encino (Oaks), San Fernando Rey de España was founded in 1797 by Father Fermín Francisco de Lasuén. It was named for King Ferdinand III of Spain (1217-1252). It is the seventeenth of twenty-one California missions.

The **altar** and **pulpit carved** from **walnut** wood are actually older than the mission itself. They were originally made in 1687 for a church in Spain, the chapel of St. Philip Neri at Ezcaray, and taken to the San Fernando Mission.

THE CONVENTO IN 1900

THE CONVENTO TODAY

In 1822, the long **Convento** was built for the Fathers and the many guests who stopped during their travels along El Camino Real.

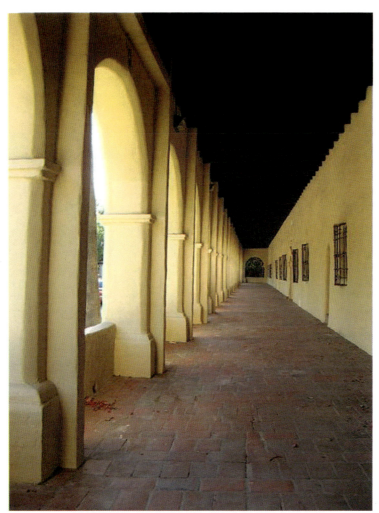
EXTERIOR CORRIDOR OF THE CONVENTO

The mission was once very **prosperous**. **Springs supplied** fresh water and **irrigation** for **agriculture**. In the early 1800s, the mission had **cattle**, **sheep**, fields of **wheat** and **beans**, 1,000 fruit trees and 32,000 grape vines. The point of the mission, of course, was to **convert** the natives to Christianity. The natives, mainly the Tataviam, came to be known as Fernandeños. They learned many skills, including how to weave, build, farm, and make wine and soap.

Mexico won its independence from Spain in 1821, and in 1834 the decision was made to close the missions. The mission lands were taken by Californian **officials** and sold. Native Americans who lived there had to leave. Then the mission buildings were used as stables (housing for horses or cattle), as a **hog** farm, and for storage.

The Northern California Gold Rush of 1848 is well known, but the first California gold was **discovered** in 1842 by a worker **digging** for wild onions in Placerita Canyon on what used to be mission land. It only took four years to find all the gold, but **greedy** diggers kept working in the hopes they would discover more. They even dug up the floors and the walls of the mission looking for gold they thought the Fathers had hidden there.

At the time of the Northern California Gold Rush, California became part of the United States and later became a state in 1850. Finally, in 1863, President Lincoln signed a law that returned all of the 21 missions to the Catholic Church.

Besides being **damaged** by hogs and gold diggers, the mission church was damaged by earthquakes in 1812 and 1971. It has since been rebuilt exactly like the church which was originally completed in 1806, and is currently an active Catholic church.

Vocabulary: Matching

A. walnut   1. _____

B. cattle   2. _____

C. sheep   3. _____

D. wheat   4. _____

E. beans   5. _____

F. hog   6. _____

VOCABULARY: MATCHING - MATCH WITHIN THE SAME COLOR

1. _____ altar
2. _____ pulpit
3. _____ to carve
4. _____ convento
5. _____ prosperous
6. _____ spring
7. _____ to supply
8. _____ irrigation
9. _____ agriculture
10. _____ to convert
11. _____ an official
12. _____ to discover
13. _____ to dig
14. _____ greedy
15. _____ to damage

A. to cut wood or stone to make an object
B. Spanish for convent = a building where religious people live
C. a raised place where a priest speaks in a church
D. rich and successful
E. a table used for a religious ceremony
F. to change or make change
G. a system of watering (giving water to) large areas
H. where water comes naturally out of the ground
I. farming (growing plants and raising animals)
J. to give something, usually something necessary
L. to break up or move away earth, snow, etc.
M. to harm or injure
N. to find something that was not known before
O. a person with a government job
P. wanting more than you need

17. Leonis Adobe

Adobe = a house made of clay and straw sun-dried bricks

23537 Calabasas Road, Calabasas, CA 91302
Hours: Wed. – Sun. 1:00 to 4:00 and Sat. 10:00-4:00 / Telephone: 818 222-6511
(CHECK FOR UPDATES)

The story of the Leonis Adobe is as wild and lawless as any legend of the Old West. It started in a small village in the mountainous Basque area between France and Spain where Michel (Miguel) Leonis was born in 1824. Like all border towns, there was plenty of opportunity for **illegal** buying and selling. Before the age of 20, Miguel already had a **prosperous** business **smuggling** goods between the two countries. Although his family was rich, well-respected, and his father even worked for the government, Miguel's dishonest activities continued for over fourteen years. Then, for reasons that are not clear, Miguel had to leave the country. Perhaps he killed someone, or was wanted by the law; maybe his parents were simply so embarrassed that they wanted to get rid of him. In any case, he ended up in Los Angeles in 1858.

He did not arrive with money. He had only his **shrewd** intelligence and large size. He was six feet four inches tall (1.92 meters). In fact, he had to work as a **shepherd** for a man named Joaquin Romero who shared a large land grant with three Chumash brothers. Joaquin was a drinker. It is possible that Miguel **took advantage** of Joaquin's condition, because he **managed** unexpectedly to buy Joaquin's **share** of the ranch for only $100.

Although $100 was worth more than it is today, even then it was surprising that Miguel got 550 acres for that **sum** (550 acres = 222.557 hectares or 2.22577 km²).

The other half of the ranch originally belonged to the Chumash brothers, one of whom was named Odon and was Chief of Humaliwo (Malibu). Odon's daughter, Espiritu, ended up **inheriting** the land. After her husband died, she was just a **defenseless widow** with a small son. She didn't have any experience running the ranch, and Miguel saw his opportunity. He married Espiritu by **contract** in the Native American style, and instantly doubled the size of his ranch. In 1860 the couple had a daughter, Marcelina. Although Miguel loved Marcelina, he was very mean to Espiritu's son, Juan Menendez, and would not even let him go into the house.

By now California was part of the United States and the Homestead Act of 1862 **allowed** anyone to take public lands by simply living in a house on the **property**. Miguel Leonis **took advantage** of this law. He found an **abandoned** adobe (house) on public lands in Calabasas and moved in. This became what we now call the Leonis Adobe.

Miguel's **greed** did not stop there. He built cheap houses on public areas next to his ranch, made workers live there as **tenants**, and then **filed claims** for the land. Of course other **settlers** would question his claims, but he fought them in court and **intimidated** them with his one hundred employees whom he **armed** with guns. Miguel Leonis was known as the "King of Calabasas." Once in 1875, he declared a war against another settler which lasted for weeks until the other man was killed.

In 1879, Miguel started **renovating** his home in the Monterey style. As you can see from the photo, the Leonis Adobe looks quite different from other Southern California historical buildings. The Monterey-style adobe was popular in Northern California.

In 1880, his daughter, Marcelina, died of smallpox. He was so upset by her death that he tried to **commit suicide** by hanging, but he was not successful. Since he had never accepted Espiritu's son as his own, he tried to find another **heir**. He had his nephew, J.B. Leonis, come from France. Although J.B. worked as an accountant for Miguel, he apparently did not want much to do with him. He started his own business in Vernon, a city southeast of Los Angeles.

In 1889, after celebrating one of his many court victories in Los Angeles, he was quite drunk when he started the long trip home. While driving through the Cahuenga pass into the Valley, he fell from his wagon and was hurt beneath its wheels. He died three days later. When he died, Miguel Leonis owned 10,000 acres (40.4685 km²) and all of his possessions were worth at least $300,000. These possessions included not only land and houses, but 3,000 cattle and $85,000 in cash.

Even though he was extremely **wealthy**, he was too **stingy** to leave his wife, Espiritu, an **inheritance**. In his will, he called her a housekeeper. She did not want to be cheated out of what was rightfully hers, so she **hired** a lawyer and won her claim to half of the Leonis property.

Unfortunately, Espiritu was later cheated out of this property by dishonest people. She hired the same lawyer who had helped her previously and finally won the case (and 3,500 acres) on September 20, 1905. A photograph was taken of her on that happy day, and this photo, as well as the black dress she was wearing, are currently on display in the Leonis Adobe. Sadly, she died less than six months later on April 10, 1906.

Espiritu's son, Juan Menendez, and his wife, Juana, lived in the adobe until two years before his death in 1924 when he sold it to Lester and Frances Agoure. The Agoures lived a fancy lifestyle, spent a lot of money, and lost the adobe to **foreclosure** in 1931. The town of Agoura just a few miles west was named after them.

From then on, the adobe went through many hands and many uses. For a time it was a restaurant, and later a retirement home. Although it was listed as the first Los Angeles Historical Monument in 1962, less than a year later there were plans to **destroy** it in order to build a shopping center. Mrs. Catherine S. Beachy fought these plans and finally bought the house herself. She then turned it over to the Leonis Adobe Association which restored it to what it was like in 1870 and opened it as a museum.

This house has been completely **furnished** in the Victorian style of the 1800s and gives us a wonderful **glimpse** into the lifestyle of that time—about one hundred fifty years ago. Farm animals (cattle, **goats**, and sheep) are still kept on the property.

IS THE LEONIS ADOBE HAUNTED?

The Agoures were the first to say that they saw ghosts in the Leonis Adobe. They thought the footsteps they heard on the second floor of the house were those of the ghost of Miguel Leonis. In the 1930s, a woman was saved from falling off a balcony as the railing broke. Hands pulled her back, but no one was there with her. At another time, a group of women saw a very tall man walk towards them and then **disappear** into an oak tree. Throughout the years, people have heard voices and sounds and have thought they have heard or seen the ghosts of Miguel and Espiritu.

WHY IS THE CITY NAMED CALABASAS?

In Spanish, the word "calabaza" means "**pumpkin**." In 1824, another Basque settler by the name of Antonio Jauregui was taking a load of pumpkins to market from his farm in Oxnard. He was heading along El Camino Real on the way to El Pueblo de Los Angeles (now the Olvera Street area of Los Angeles). He didn't get very far. His horses saw a **rattlesnake** and were so frightened that they upset the cart and all the pumpkins fell out and broke to pieces. His damaged produce was worthless, so he simply left all the broken pumpkins where they were and went home. Several months later, pumpkin plants started growing on that spot. The pumpkin plants became a landmark and the area became known as "Pumpkins" or Calabasas.

VOCABULARY: MATCHING - MATCH WITHIN THE SAME COLOR

Set #1

1. _____ illegal
2. _____ prosperous
3. _____ to smuggle
4. _____ shrewd
5. _____ shepherd
6. _____ to take advantage
7. _____ to manage
8. _____ share
9. _____ sum
10. _____ to inherit
11. _____ defenseless
12. _____ widow
13. _____ contract
14. _____ to allow
15. _____ property
16. _____ to abandon
17. _____ greed
18. _____ tenant

A. rich and successful
B. to use a person or situation to help oneself
C. against the law
D. a person who herds (goes with/takes care of) sheep
E. intelligent, practical, and sometimes tricky
F. to illegally take from one country to another
G. to get something from someone after his/her death
H. an amount of money; also x + x = (this word)
I. a part that someone owns
J. to succeed in doing a difficult thing
K. a woman after the death of her husband
M. not able to protect oneself
N. someone who pays rent for where he/she lives
O. a desire, or want, for more than one needs
P. to permit someone to do something
Q. to leave a place or person and never go back
R. a legal agreement, usually written.
S. what someone owns

Set #2

1. _____ file a claim
2. _____ settler
3. _____ to intimidate
4. _____ to arm
5. _____ to renovate
6. _____ commit suicide
7. _____ heir
8. _____ wealthy
9. _____ stingy
10. _____ inheritance
11. _____ to hire
12. _____ foreclosure
13. _____ to destroy
14. _____ to furnish
15. _____ glimpse
16. _____ goat
17. _____ to disappear

A. a person who begins to live in a place
B. to kill oneself
C. to give someone arms (guns, etc.)
D. to repair something, usually a building
E. to ask for legally
F. to make a person afraid to do something
G. the person who gets something when another dies
H. not wanting to give even though he/she has enough
J. what is received from someone who dies
K. to give someone a job
L. rich
M. noun: when a person can't pay for a loan, the bank takes away the property, such as a house
N. to put furniture (chairs, etc.) and objects in
O. to not be seen anymore; to go away
P. to damage completely; to tear down
Q. a quick look
R. ⟶

DISCUSSION AND CRITICAL THINKING

1. Michel (Miguel) Leonis was a shrewd man. Do you think all of his killing and cheating was worth it? Why or why not?
2. Role play/debate: Miguel and Espiritu Leonis argue about the inheritance.
3. Do you believe in ghosts? Why or why not?

18. Andres Pico Adobe
Also Called Romulo Pico Adobe

10940 Sepulveda Blvd., Mission Hills, CA 91345
Monday 10:00 A.M. to 3:00 P.M. and Every Third Sunday/Telephone: (818) 365-7810
(CHECK FOR UPDATES)

There are a few other important adobes in the San Fernando Valley. "Adobe" is a building made of clay and straw bricks dried in the sun, and this was the method used for building in the early days of Southern California.

The Andres Pico Adobe is the oldest home in the Valley, and the second oldest home in Los Angeles (the first is on Olvera Street). This house was built on mission lands by and probably for the Native Americans. In 1845, after mission lands were taken from the church and sold, the Pico family moved into this house. Pico is a very famous name. Pío Pico was the last Mexican Governor of California. Andre was his brother. Andre Pico's adopted son, Romulo, and his wife, Catarina, lived in the adobe and added a second floor in 1873. It was old and damaged when Dr. Mark Harrington bought it in 1930. He found the original tiles under a wood floor. Tiles like these were made only before 1834, so we know the house is from that date or before.

The Orcutt Ranch
Also Called Rancho Sombra del Roble

23600 Roscoe Blvd., West Hills, CA 91304
Open Daily from Sunrise to Sunset / Telephone (818) 346-7449
(CHECK FOR UPDATES)

Called the ranch in the **shade** of the oak (Rancho Sombra del Roble), this was the vacation home of William and Mary Orcutt. After graduating from Stanford University with a degree in **geology**, William Orcutt worked for oil companies. At a time when it was not common to use geology in the oil industry, Mr. Orcutt used geologic **principles** for oil development with such success that oil companies started to require such studies. He was honored for his work in the industry with two cities named Orcutt: one in Southern California and another in Colorado. During his exploration of the area for the industry, in 1901 he **discovered** the first prehistoric bones in the La Brea Tar Pits, and a prehistoric **coyote** was named after him: Canis Orcutti.

William and Mary wanted a Spanish mission-style ranch home, so they had one built in 1926 to seem as though it had come from the earlier mission era. They used designs from the Southwest and Native American culture. A Native American symbol seen all over the ranch is the swastika, which at that time was commonly used for good luck. Since the beginning of time, cultures all over the world have used the swastika. Only after the **adoption** of this symbol by Nazi Germany did it become so hated.

Twenty-four acres (9.7 hectares or 0.097 km²) of citrus orchards, oak trees, and flower gardens surround the Orcutt Ranch. One oak tree is more than 700 years old and is 33 feet (10 meters) around. It is a pleasant place to spend the day. One weekend in July, the citrus orchards are open to the public. You may pick an entire grocery bag full of Valencia oranges or white grapefruit for only a couple of dollars.

VOCABULARY: MATCHING

A. shade
B. geology
C. principle
D. to discover
E. coyote
F. adoption

1. _____ →
2. _____ a decision to have or use something as one's own
3. _____ an area without direct sun that is cooler
4. _____ the study of rocks, minerals, and the earth (soil)
5. _____ to find something that was not known before
6. _____ an idea or rule about what is right or wrong

DISCUSSION AND CRITICAL THINKING

1. Although Mr. and Mrs. Orcutt lived in the Mid-Wilshire/Korea Town area of Los Angeles not far from the La Brea Tar Pits, the couple liked to take time off to spend on their ranch outside the city. Do you think it is important to spend time in nature? Why or why not?
2. The world population has more than doubled since 1960. When the Orcutts had their ranch, the Valley was mostly trees, orchards, and land for sheep and cattle. Before that, the Spanish had named the Valley "Encino" after all the oaks that they found there. Clearly, wild places and nature have suffered as the world population has grown. Do you think this presents a problem? Why or why not? If so, what can we do about it?

AN OAK TREE

VOCABULARY REVIEW PUZZLE #1

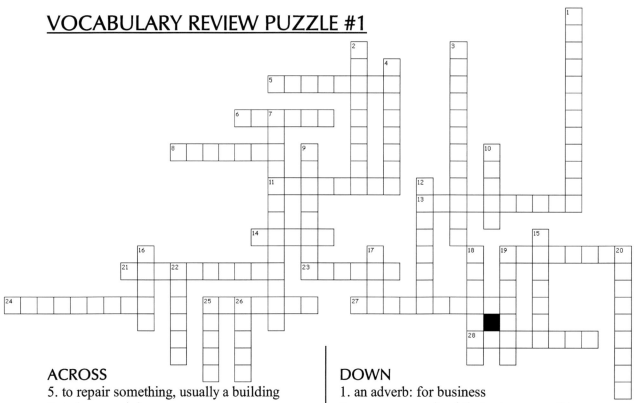

ACROSS
5. to repair something, usually a building
6. to harm or injure
8. not existing anymore
11. a natural item that is used
13. the study of knowledge, life, and what is good or bad
14. a person owned by another and forced to work
19. lack of respect because you have done wrong
21. rich and successful
23. to stay the same
24. an idea or rule about what is right or wrong
25. a story, usually for entertainment, that is not true
27. a place where people begin to live
28. a decision to have or use something as one's own

DOWN
1. an adverb: for business
2. a person or animal that eats or uses things others have thrown away
3. payment for something given, done, or suffered
4. the traditions of a group
7. thinking that things are more important than art, religion, etc.
9. to find something that was not known before
10. to permit someone to do something
12. an official agreement or acceptance
15. a sticky, naturally occurring, black substance
16. a desire for more than you need
17. to give someone a job
18. against the law
19. to damage completely
20. to accept and understand; also, realize you know
22. to have pain, a bad experience, or an illness
25. to start a town, business, or organization
26. to say you own something or have a right to it

HINTS

A list of the words (and a few hints) for the crossword puzzle on the previous page.

adoption
allow
approval
asphalt
claim
commercially
compensation
damage
destroy
discover
dishonor
extinct
fiction
found
greed
heritage
hire
illegal
material = of money or things rather than mind or spirit
materialistic = thinking that things are more important than art, religion, etc.
philosophy
principle
prosperous
recognize
remains = what is left
remain = to stay the same
renovate
resource
scavenger
settlement
slave
suffer

19. The Gene Autry National Center

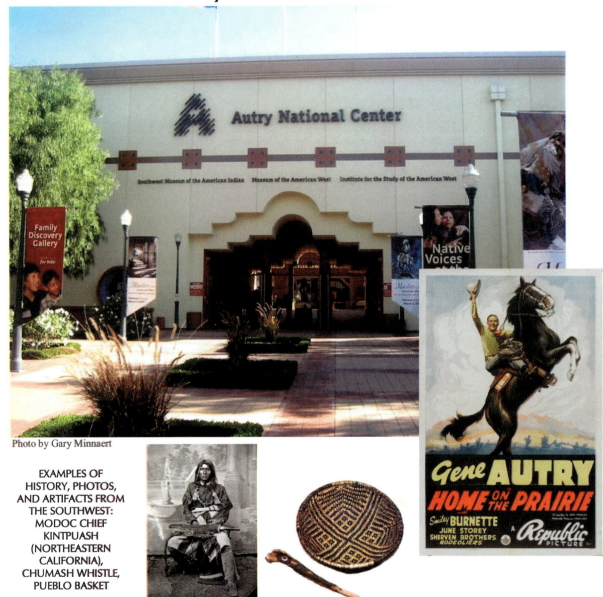

Photo by Gary Minnaert

EXAMPLES OF HISTORY, PHOTOS, AND ARTIFACTS FROM THE SOUTHWEST: MODOC CHIEF KINTPUASH (NORTHEASTERN CALIFORNIA), CHUMASH WHISTLE, PUEBLO BASKET

SOUTHWEST MUSEUM OF THE AMERICAN INDIAN
MUSEUM OF THE AMERICAN WEST
INSTITUTE FOR THE STUDY OF THE AMERICAN WEST
4700 Western Heritage Way, Los Angeles, CA 90027
Telephone: (323) 667-2000 (CHECK FOR UPDATES)
Closed on Mon./Tues. – Fri.: 10 A.M. – 4 P.M./Sat. – Sun.: 10 A.M. – 5 P.M.

This museum explores the history of various cultures and exhibits **artifacts** from all the cultures that made up the American West. There is no other museum like it. There are often special **exhibits** showing Native American baskets and artifacts, migrants searching for a better life, information about the Sioux battles, and antique guns.

Gene Autry was a **yodeling** cowboy, singer, song-writer, actor, television star, World War II veteran, and the **founder** of the Autry National Center. He wrote or co-wrote over 300 songs, received numerous awards, and is the only performer with five stars on the Hollywood Walk of Fame, one for each category: Recording, Motion Pictures, Television, Radio, and Live Theater. His horse, Champion, was a constant co-star and for each movie the horse's name was posted along with Gene's, above the names of all the other actors and actresses. In fact, Gene had several horses, all with the name Champion. After their movie careers, the horses retired to his ranch in Newhall, north of Los Angeles. In 1940, Lindy Champion became the first horse ever to fly from California to New York on an airplane. Touring Champion's **hoof** prints are at TCL Grauman's Chinese Theatre in Hollywood right next to Gene's handprints. Champion even received fan mail—thousands of letters each month!

Photos by Joseph Kane

TOGETHER IN THE MOVIE *OH, SUSANNA !* 1936
Gene Autry 1907 - 1998

Gene Autry was a hard worker. He performed two shows a day every day – no rest for weekends – and he did this for 65 or 85 days without a break. He had his own **philosophy**. The following are his "Ten Cowboy **Commandments**."

1. The Cowboy must never shoot first, hit a smaller man, or **take** unfair **advantage**.
2. He must never go back on his word, or a **trust confided** in him.
3. He must always tell the truth.
4. He must be **gentle** with children, the **elderly**, and animals.
5. He must not **advocate** or **possess racially** or religiously **intolerant** ideas.
6. He must help people in **distress**.
7. He must be a good worker.
8. He must keep himself clean in thought, speech, action, and personal habits.
9. He must respect women, parents, and his nation's laws.
10. The Cowboy is a **patriot**.

VOCABULARY: MATCHING - MATCH WITHIN THE SAME COLOR

Some of these words appeared in previous chapters. Do you remember them?

1. _____ artifact
2. _____ exhibit
3. _____ basket
4. _____ migrant
5. _____ to yodel
6. _____ founder
7. _____ hoof
8. _____ philosophy
9. _____ take advantage
10. _____ commandment
11. _____ trust
12. _____ to confide
13. _____ gentle
14. _____ elderly
15. _____ to possess
16. _____ racially
17. _____ intolerant
18. _____ distress
19. _____ patriot

A. to sing in a very high tone, up and down
B. a person who goes to another place to find work
C. a person who starts a town or business
D. a historically important object
E. a container made of woven plants
F. show
G. to tell someone a secret
H. a belief in the honesty of someone
I. to use a person or situation to help oneself
J. a rule to do what is right (10 rules in the Bible)
K. the study of knowledge, truth, and life
L. a horse's foot
M. to have or own
N. old, or old people
O. adverb: of a race, or group of people
P. in danger, or in a sad or difficult situation
Q. not accepting anything different
R. a person who loves his or her country
S. kind and careful not to harm or hurt

DISCUSSION AND CRITICAL THINKING

1. What do you think of Gene Autry's "Ten Commandments"? Would you like to adopt any of his commandments? Why or why not?
2. Are there any commandments you would like to add to Gene Autry's? Do you live by any principles?
3. Why is it important to be a good worker?
4. What does it mean to be a patriot? How can you express your love for your country?
5. Role play: Imagine you are either Gene Autry or Miguel Leonis. You are discussing principles and how to live life. Gene Autry doesn't like the way Miguel intimidates those who want to settle on land near his. What does Miguel say?
6. What would you like to see at the Gene Autry Museum?

_____
_____
_____

20. The Los Angeles Zoo and Botanical Gardens

5333 Zoo Drive, Los Angeles, CA 90027
Open Daily from 10:00 A.M. – 5:00 P.M. / Telephone (323) 644-4200
(CHECK FOR UPDATES)

- **Kelly:** What are you doing this weekend?
- **David:** I'm going to the zoo. Do you want to come?
- **Kelly:** No way. It's so sad to see animals in **cages**.
- **David:** Without zoos, the California condor would be **extinct**!
- **Kelly:** Keeping birds in cages is *not* my idea of **conserving** nature.
- **David:** You don't **get** it. The whole point is to **release** them. In 1980, there were fewer than 25 in the **wild**. They **captured** them all for this **awesome breeding** program. Now they've got over 400, and over 200 are free!
- **Kelly:** Are you serious? Only 400? After thirty years? What's so awesome about that?
- **David:** Hey, *we're* the problem, not the breeding program. We're taking their **habitat**, and **lead bullets** often kill them.
- **Kelly:** Some idiot **shot** them!
- **David:** No, the birds *ate* the bullets. Condors are **scavengers**, and if they eat a dead animal with a lead bullet in it, they get lead **poisoning**.
- **Kelly:** Lead bullets should be **banned**.
- **David:** They *are* **banned** in parts of California, and will be banned everywhere in California by 2019, but condors are still eating lead bullets.
- **Kelly:** Can I see a California condor at the Los Angeles Zoo?
- **David:** No. We can't disturb the breeding program. But you can see an Andean condor. And there's a new elephant exhibit, plus the meerkats. I love the meerkats. . . .

123

The California condor is one of the rarest birds in the world, and is the largest bird in North America. Although they are **endangered** now, they used to live in many parts of the United States. By 1900, they could be **found** only in Southern California.

Their wing**span** is 9 ½ feet (almost 3 meters) and they weigh about 23 pounds (about 10.4 kilograms). They do their **duty** for the **environment** by cleaning up dead animals. Adult birds, which live as long as 60 years, are all black except for their heads and the white feathers under their wings. Young birds have black heads. As they **mature**, their featherless heads turn from black to pink, yellow, or orange. These birds are **monogamous**, and they lay only one egg every two years. Both the mother and father take care of the chicks. They are social birds and like to stay in groups. They can be seen sailing on the wind in the Grand Canyon and occasionally in parts of California. As you can see in the picture, all the birds have **tags**, numbers, and transmitters, so we can **keep track of** them.

Condor Photos by Michael Quinn

Meerkats are from southern Africa. They are fun to watch. You will find them near the entrance of the zoo. They live in groups and work together. One always stands **guard** looking at the sky. If it sees a dangerous bird, or even an airplane, it will chatter to the others and they will all run to hide.

VOCABULARY: MATCHING - MATCH WITHIN THE SAME COLOR

1. _____ cage
2. _____ extinct
3. _____ to conserve
4. _____ to get
5. _____ to release
6. _____ wild
7. _____ to capture
8. _____ awesome
9. _____ to breed
10. _____ habitat
11. _____ lead
12. _____ bullet
13. _____ to shoot (past=shot)
14. _____ scavenger
15. _____ poisoning
16. _____ to ban
17. _____ endangered
18. _____ to find (past=found)
19. _____ span
20. _____ duty
21. _____ environment
22. _____ to mature
23. _____ monogamous
24. _____ tag
25. _____ to keep track of
26. _____ guard

A. to keep something from being damaged
B. after being trapped, to allow to be free; let go
C. this word has many meanings; here=understand
D. not existing anymore; all are dead
E. a place with bars or wires to keep animals
F. to keep animals in order to make baby animals
G. in nature, without control by people
H. to catch, trap, and make a prisoner
I. very good, impressive, or serious
J. the natural place where a plant or animal lives
K. person / animal that uses what others throw away
L. a heavy, soft metal (Pb)
M. to use a gun
N. illness caused by eating something that can kill
O. a small piece of metal shot from a gun
P. to get by looking for
Q. the distance from one end to the other
R. something you have to do; responsibility
S. to legally or officially say a person can't do it
T. in a dangerous situation; it might soon be extinct
U. someone who has the job of protecting others
V. a small note to show name, address, or cost
W. to grow into an adult
X. the air, land and water around where we live
Y. to pay attention and know what is happening
Z. having only one partner or mate

TRUE OR FALSE

1. _____ Condors kill animals for food.
2. _____ Condors lay only one egg every two years.
3. _____ At one time there were no California condors in the wild.
4. _____ Condors are the biggest birds in the world.
5. _____ Meerkats are social animals.

DISCUSSION AND CRITICAL THINKING

1. Do you think we should make sure California condors and other animals do not become extinct? Why or why not? What can humans gain from animals?
2. Role play or debate: Half of the class will take the part of David, who thinks zoos are important, and half of the class will take the part of Kelly.

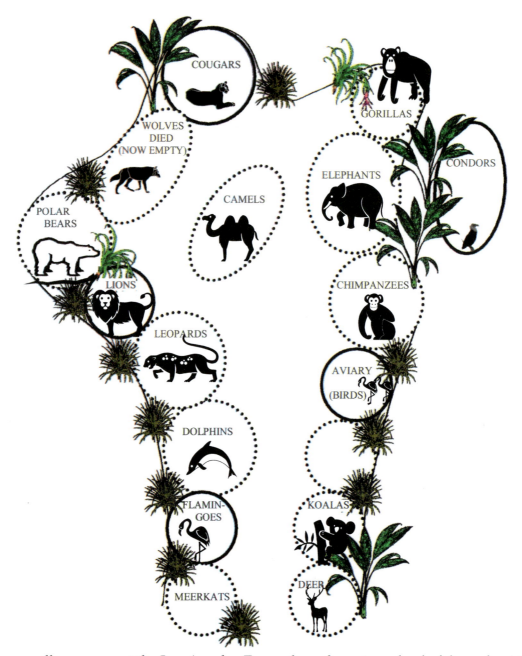

You are all managers at the Los Angeles Zoo and you have to make decisions about the following issues. Discuss until you all agree.

1. The zoo will have to buy two new types of animals. You decide which.
2. The coyotes from Griffith Park have attacked the meerkats. You need to move them into a safer area (solid line). Be careful not to move other defenseless animals into an area that is not safe.
3. The koalas had baby koalas this spring. They need a bigger area, but you must be careful to put them in an area with eucalyptus.
4. You are going to trade one animal with the Bronx Zoo in New York City. Which animal will you give up, and which will you ask for?
5. Note: The dolphins and polar bears have pools and need them. The elephants can't be moved because their enclosure was just built especially for them.

DISCUSSION AND CRITICAL THINKING

You may use these grammar structures:

We should (verb) . . . . We must (verb). . . . This animal/These animals must (verb)
This animal has to (verb) . . . . These animals have to (verb) . . . .
This animal doesn't have to (verb) . . . . These animals don't have to (verb) . . . .
If we _____, _____ will _____.
Comparative adjectives: _____ is bigg**er**/**more** active **than** _____.

All zoo managers must agree on the decisions. When you all agree, fill in the map.

21. The Griffith Observatory

Photo by Matthew Field

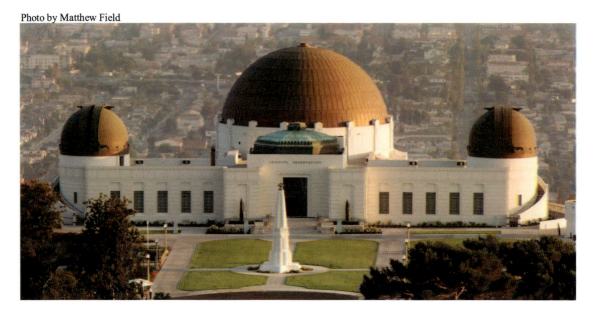

2800 East Observatory Road, Los Angeles, CA 90027
Tues. to Fri. 12:00-10:00 P.M.; Sat. & Sun. 10:00-10:00 P.M. (CHECK FOR UPDATES)
Telephone: (213) 473-0800

Griffith Park, covering 4, 210 acres (more than 1703.7 hectares or 17 square kilometers), is the largest **wild** park inside a city in the United States. As well as being home to the Los Angeles Zoo and the Gene Autry Museum, the park also includes wild areas that are almost unchanged from the days when only the Native Americans lived here. If you hike one of the many **trails**, you may see deer, coyotes, **hawks**, and snakes.

Born in South Wales in 1850, Griffith Jenkins Griffith **emigrated** to the United States when he was only 15 years old. He ended up making a great deal of money mining gold in California. In 1882, he **settled** in Los Angeles and bought ranch land. He gave this land to the city of Los Angeles in 1896 on many conditions: It would be used as a park for the people of Los Angeles and it would include a Greek **amphitheater**, an **observatory**, and a hall of science. He said, "I consider it my **obligation** to make Los Angeles a happier, cleaner, and finer city. I wish to pay my **debt** of **duty** in this way to the community in which I have **prospered**."

Griffith wanted to make sure the public had the opportunity to look through a telescope. The 12-inch Zeiss telescope in the eastern **dome** of the observatory is **available** to the public for nighttime viewing. More people have seen the moon, planets, and stars through this telescope than any other telescope in the world. There are also three **solar** telescopes in the observatory. On clear days, they give three different views of the sun. In addition, coin-operated telescopes around the building give visitors a view of the city below.

The observatory also offers various shows which are given throughout the day. Check *http://www.griffithobservatory.org* for the exact times and subjects.

VOCABULARY: MATCHING - MATCH WITHIN THE SAME COLOR

Some of these words we have covered in other chapters. Others have been in the readings although we have not focused on them. Do you remember these words?

1. _____wild
2. _____trail
3. _____hawk
4. _____to settle
5. _____amphitheater
6. _____observatory
7. _____obligation
8. _____debt
9. _____duty
10. _____to prosper
11. _____dome
12. _____available
13. _____solar

A. a large bird that kills to eat
B. to begin to live in an area
C. in nature, without control by people
D. large round place outside with seats for performances
E. a path (small road) in places where not many people go
F. a special building for watching the moon, stars, etc.
G. money that you owe (have to pay back to someone)
H. something you have to do; responsibility; duty
I. a round roof
J. ready to have, buy, or use
K. having to do with the sun
L. to become rich and successful
M. what you must do legally, or morally (to be good)

TRUE OR FALSE

1. ____Griffith J. Griffith made his money by ranching.
2. ____Griffith J. Griffith was born in the United States.
3. ____Griffith J. Griffith gave his land to the city to use for any purpose.
4. ____Wild animals live in Griffith Park.
5. ____ All of the Griffith Park telescopes can only be used at night.

DISCUSSION AND CRITICAL THINKING

1. Why did Griffith J. Griffith feel that he was in debt?
2. Do you think he made an important contribution to Los Angeles? Why or why not? Do you think the city could have made better use of the land?
3. Do you think it is important to have wild areas in the world? Why or why not?
4. Griffith J. Griffith was rich. Do you think all people, rich or poor, have a debt to society or nature? Why or why not?
5. Is there any way for people who are not rich to help the earth or society? How? As we discuss, jot down some notes:

_____

_____

_____

22. The Getty Museums

The J. Paul Getty Center
1200 Getty Center Drive, Los Angeles, CA 90049-1687
Tues.–Fri. 10 A.M.–5:30 P.M.; Sat. 10 A.M.–9:00 P.M.; Sun. 10 A.M.–5:30 P.M.
Admission is free, but parking is not. Telephone (310) 440-7330
(CHECK FOR UPDATES)

The J. Paul Getty Center was designed by the architect Richard Meier. This newer, larger museum is where you should go to see all kinds of **paintings**, **sculptures**, **drawings**, and photographs. There are also films, **performances**, **lectures**, and various other activities. Admission is free.

When visiting an art museum or an art gallery, you will see artwork in various media, which include paintings, drawings, prints, or sculptures. On the following pages, you will find a detailed explanation of each medium, but you don't need fancy language to enjoy art. You can use the word "piece" to describe any form of artwork.

- **Abdullah:** Are you enjoying yourself?
- **Tomoyo:** Yes. I really like this piece.

IRISES
BY VINCENT VAN GOGH
AN OIL PAINTING AT THE J. PAUL GETTY CENTER

MEDIA (singular = medium) AT A GALLERY OR AN ART MUSEUM

Different types of paintings:
- **oil** (usually on canvas, but also on wood) – The color is mixed in an oil base; oil colors are usually more brilliant than acrylic. Oil takes a couple of days to dry.
- **acrylic** (usually on canvas, but also on wood) – The color is mixed in a synthetic (not natural) resin which is water-soluble and dries faster than oil paint. In the 1940s, the original idea for acrylic paints came from artists using car paint.
- **egg tempera** (usually on wood) – Egg yolk is mixed with color.
- **watercolor** – The color is mixed with water. This is not as permanent as oil or acrylic (it can fade, or lose its color).
- **encaustic** (usually on wood) – The color is mixed with wax.

Pastels – Gum- or oil-based chalk used for drawing. The result sometimes looks like painting.

Drawings – Usually made with chalk, pen, or pencil.

A SAINT ON HORSEBACK
BY CIMA DA CONEGLIANO
A RED CHALK DRAWING
AT THE J. PAUL GETTY CENTER

131

Different types of prints:
Prints are multiple copies of pictures made by pressing ink (from stone, wood, metal, etc.) onto paper; the copies are usually mirror-image, except for screen prints and giclée.

Type 1: the ink on the surface
- **lithographs** – Designs are drawn with greasy pencils on stone or metal. Oil-based ink sticks to the greasy areas. Water keeps the ink away from the stone, or the metal plate (plate=smooth flat sheet of metal, plastic, etc).
- **woodcuts** – Designs are cut on wood. The ink is put on the surface of the design and transferred to paper.
- **Screen prints** – Designs are made by blocking areas on a screen. Ink is pressed through the screen in the unblocked areas.
- **giclée** – A high-quality print made from a digital ink-jet printer.
- **monoprint** - A single print made by painting on a plate (no multiples).

Type 2: intaglio - The ink is rubbed into cut areas; the surface is cleaned.
- **engravings** – cut into copper or brass with a tool called a burin
- **drypoint** – scratched into copper, plastic, etc., with a needle
- **etchings** – designs cut by acid into the unprotected parts of a metal plate

sculptures – three dimensional artwork usually of stone, metal, or wood

ceramics – made of clay, terracotta, or earth

functional (clay bowls, cups, vases, etc., that can be used for a purpose)

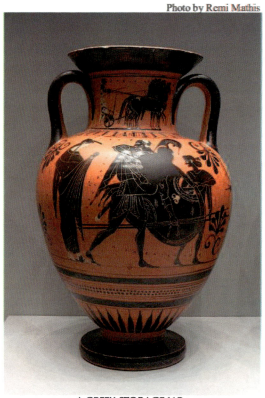

Photo by Remi Mathis

non-functional (like clay sculptures, used only to look at)

A GREEK STORAGE JAR
TERRACOTTA
AT THE GETTY VILLA

Photo by Bobak Ha'Eri

The Getty Villa near Malibu
**17985 Pacific Coast Highway, Pacific Palisades, CA 90272
Wednesday–Monday 10:00 A.M.–5:00 P.M.
(Although tickets are free, a timed reservation is needed, and parking is not free.
Go to http://tickets.getty.edu/ or www.getty.edu/visit)**

This villa exhibits Greek, Roman, and Etruscan **antiquities**.

J. Paul Getty once said, "The beauty one can find in art is one of the **pitifully** few real and **lasting products** of human **endeavor**." His dream was to recreate the ancient Villa dei Papiri which was **found,** in the 18th century, far under the **ground** in Herculaneum. Herculaneum and Pompeii were **destroyed** by the volcano Vesuvius in 79 C.E. Paul Getty hired Stephen Garrett, an **architect** and **consultant**, to build a villa like it so people could go there and have the feeling of living long ago. It was finished in 1974. Unfortunately, J. Paul Getty died in 1976 and never saw it.

If you would like to step back into time, to 79 C.E, for a day and enjoy 44,000 works of art from **ancient** Greece, Rome, and **Etruria**, this museum is for you.

A BRONZE SCULPTURE
AT THE GETTY VILLA

Photo by Dave Hill & Margie Kleerup

VOCABULARY: MATCHING - MATCH WITHIN THE SAME COLOR

1. _____ painting
2. _____ sculpture
3. _____ drawing
4. _____ performance
5. _____ lecture
6. _____ antiquity
7. _____ pitifully
8. _____ lasting
9. _____ product
10. _____ endeavor
11. _____ find (past=found)
12. _____ ground
13. _____ to destroy
14. _____ architect
15. _____ consultant
16. _____ ancient
17. _____ Etruria

A. a picture made with a pen or pencil
B. a picture made with a brush and colored liquid
C. something done for an audience (people watching)
D. a long serious talk, usually to a group
E. a 3-dimensional work of art in metal, wood, clay
F. sadly; making you feel sympathy-bad for another
G. something made in ancient times-a long time ago
H. something that is grown or made or sold
I. serious activity for a purpose
J. to get by looking for
K. existing for a long time; still here from long ago
L. an ancient culture in central Italy before 300 B.C.E.
M. a person with a job to design buildings
N. a person with a job to give advice
O. very old, before 476 C.E. when Rome fell
P. land, the surface of the earth
Q. to damage completely

DISCUSSION AND CRITICAL THINKING

1. J. Paul Getty wanted to create a villa where people could go and have the feeling of living in ancient times. Have you ever wanted to go back in time and live in a particular time in the past? If so, what historical time would you like to visit? Why?
2. J. Paul Getty said, "The beauty one can find in art is one of the pitifully few real and lasting products of human endeavor."
   a. Do you agree or disagree with him?
   b. If you agree, explain why art is so important.
   c. In your opinion, what is the purpose of art?
   d. Does art have to be beautiful? If not, what does it have to be?
   e. What is your favorite kind of art?
   f. In your opinion, what is beautiful? Name some things that you think are beautiful.
   g. Is art necessary? If so, why? If not, why not?
   h. He said, "one of the few." Can you think of anything else that man produces that is lasting?
   i. If you disagree, explain how many things you think are lasting and important.
3. J. Paul Getty was a very rich man. What do you think money meant to him?
4. If you had a lot of money, what would you do with it? Answer: I would . . . .
5. If you could leave one thing in the world, what would it be?
6. Do you think animals can create art? If you think so, give some examples. If you think they cannot, explain why not.

23. The Beaches

LEO CARRILLO BEACH

There are so many beaches in Southern California that you can choose one depending on what **mood** you are in. Go to *http://watchthewater.org/beach_locator.cfm* where you can check the **facilities** of each beach (for example: bike paths, bus stop, picnic areas, volleyball, surfing, etc.). Here are only a few of the great beaches:

- Venice Beach – This is definitely the beach to go to if you are in a crazy **mood**. Street **performers** line the sidewalk and vendors sell interesting **souvenirs**. This beach also has a bike **path** (you can rent a bike), restaurants, showers, restrooms, and it is also good for surfing and playing volleyball.
- Santa Monica Beach – Although this doesn't pop up on the beach locator, this is one of the best beaches for **sunbathing** and relaxing. It has the Santa Monica Pier, swimming, surfing, fishing, volleyball and biking. Nearby is the wonderful Third Street Promenade where cars are **prohibited**. You can walk, **window-shop**, eat in great restaurants, and watch **fascinating** people go by.
- Cabrillo Beach in Los Angeles is the only beach listed by the Watch Tower for **tide pools**, but you can also see them at the Santa Monica Pier and Leo Carrillo Beach in Malibu. You can see **starfish**, **anemones**, **shells**, and other sea creatures, but **you must not take home anything you find on the beach.** It is prohibited.

Check *http://www.saltwatertides.com/pickpred.html* to see when the low tides will make tide pools. Select the region, then the area (Port Hueneme is a good choice for Leo Carrillo Beach). On the list, choose the date and how many days you want to see the tides. You will get a schedule of high and low tides.

135

VOCABULARY: MATCHING

Match the pictures with the words:

A. starfish   B. anemone   C. shell

1. _____   2. _____   3. _____

A. mood
B. facility
C. performer
D. souvenir
E. path
F. sunbathing
G. to prohibit
H. window-shop
I. fascinating
J. tide
K. pool

1. _____ to look in store windows without buying
2. _____ a small area of water
3. _____ something you have to make you remember a trip, etc.
4. _____ a way, like a very small road, created for walking or biking
5. _____ to say something is against the law or not allowed
6. _____ a general feeling
7. _____ the everyday rise and fall of the water in the ocean
8. _____ staying in the sun for a tan or for fun
9. _____ a service or building used for a purpose
10. _____ someone who does something for an audience
11. _____ very interesting

STREET PERFORMER ON VENICE BEACH

GO, TO GO, AND GOING TO THE BEACH

There are three types of verbs which use another verb after them.

AUXILIARY (HELPING) VERBS – NO "TO"!
We <u>should</u> <u>go</u> to the beach.

VERBS THAT TAKE "TO" BEFORE ANOTHER VERB
I <u>want</u> <u>to go</u> to the beach.

VERBS THAT TAKE THE "ING" FORM OF THE VERB
She <u>enjoys</u> <u>going</u> to the beach.

VERB PATTERN	VERBS THAT FOLLOW THE PATTERN
MODALS AUXILIARY VERB + MAIN VERB **He <u>might go</u> to the beach.**	will may would might can should could must
VERB + OBJECT + MAIN VERB	let (My mother let me go to the beach.) make (My boss made me work overtime.)
VERB + TO + VERB **They <u>plan to go</u> to the beach.** * Sometimes "ing" is used like a noun: I chose visiting a museum over spending time at the beach. I promised going to La Brea Tar Pits would be better than shopping.	ask choose* decide* expect hope* learn manage need plan promise* refuse want would like would love
VERB + VERB + ING **I <u>enjoy going</u> to the beach.**	admit appreciate avoid consider dislike enjoy finish imagine keep postpone quit recommend suggest
VERB + TO + VERB OR VERB + VERB + ING <u>WITH THE SAME MEANING</u> **I like <u>going to</u> the beach.** **I like <u>to go</u> to the beach.**	begin continue hate like love prefer start
VERB + TO + VERB OR VERB + VERB + ING <u>WITH A DIFFERENT MEANING</u>* *Examples: I <u>remembered to go</u> to the beach. (I went.) I <u>remember going</u> to the beach. (I remember that I went.) Let's <u>stop to eat</u> (we want to eat). Let's <u>stop driving</u> (no more driving). Let's <u>stop driving to eat</u>.	forget regret remember stop try

Don't try to remember all of these at once. Note that the modals use the simple base verb; remember a few with "to + verb" (ask, decide, need, plan, want) and a few with "to + verb + ing" (enjoy, recommend, suggest).

PRACTICE GO, TO GO, OR GOING TO THE BEACH

1. He admitted *going to the beach.*
2. She avoided *going to the beach.*
3. They appreciated *going to the beach.*
4. He asked
5. I can
6. She always chooses
7. You should consider
8. They couldn't
9. We decided
10. She dislikes
11. We all enjoy
12. Don't expect
13. She made her brother
14. They finished
15. I hope
16. Imagine
17. I would like to keep
18. He always likes
19. They managed
20. I might
21. You must
22. I don't need
23. You should plan
24. They promised
25. Never quit
26. They recommend
27. She refuses
28. Should I _____ ?
29. He suggested
30. Do you want _____ ?
31. If it's sunny, they will
32. When she was a child, she would
33. He would like
34. His mother let him

LEO CARRILLO BEACH: STARFISH IN A TIDE POOL

24. Blue Jeans

Blue jeans are a part of American history. The key players were two **immigrants**, Levi Strauss, an immigrant from Germany, and Jacob Davis, an immigrant from Latvia.

Like all inventions, blue jeans were **designed** to solve a problem. A **tailor** named Jacob Davis had a **customer** who continually **tore** the pockets of his pants. Davis decided to put **metal rivets** on the pockets and on other places that needed strengthening. The idea worked and these pants became very popular. He began to worry that someone might **steal** his idea. Taking out a **patent** was the only thing to do, but he didn't have the **required** $68. He decided to ask the businessman who **supplied** him with material.

Levi Strauss had a store in San Francisco that sold **fabrics**, clothing, and other such **items**. Davis asked if Strauss would like **to share** the patent on these riveted pants. Strauss thought it was an excellent idea, and on May 20, 1873, they got their patent. Unfortunately, no one knows the exact date these pants were first **manufactured** because all records were lost in the 1906 San Francisco earthquake and fire.

Levi Strauss put his name on them, but Jacob Davis **managed** the two factories in San Francisco. The strong material, denim, came from Amoskeag Mill in Manchester, New Hampshire, which was a mill known for excellent fabrics.

Blue jeans might seem to be a stylish fashion statement, but historically they have been strong clothes worn by cowboys, miners, and other workers, especially in the American West. Originally they were called "overalls" because they were worn over clothes in order to **protect** them. Later people started wearing the pants alone. According to the Merriam-Webster dictionary, the first known use of the words "blue jeans" was in 1901. After the patent **expired** in 1890, many companies started making riveted pants.

VOCABULARY: MATCHING - MATCH WITHIN THE SAME COLOR

1. _____ immigrant
2. _____ to design
3. _____ tailor
4. _____ customer
5. _____ to tear (past=torn)
6. _____ metal

A. a person who buys
B. a person who goes into another country to live
C. a person with the job of making clothes
D. to rip (break) paper or fabric
E. something solid, hard, and shiny like gold or iron
F. to create or plan for a purpose

7. _____ rivet
8. _____ to steal
9. _____ patent
10. _____ to require
11. _____ to supply
12. _____ fabric

G. a license that says only you can make something
H. to give something, usually something necessary
I. to take a thing that someone else owns
J. a metal piece to connect things
K. cloth for sewing, often called material
L. to need

13. _____ item
14. _____ to share
15. _____ to manufacture
16. _____ to manage
17. _____ to protect
18. _____ to expire

M. to use or own with others or another person
N. to come to the end of a contract or time to use
O. to keep from harm or damage
P. to make with machines
Q. a thing
R. to direct; also, to succeed in doing something

DISCUSSION AND CRITICAL THINKING

1. Do you think your jeans are the most important part of your wardrobe (clothing)?
2. Did you know that Levi Strauss jeans were the first jeans?
3. Will you be more likely to buy Levi Strauss jeans now that you know the history?
4. What brand of jeans do you like? Why?
5. What influences you (makes you change your mind) when you buy jeans?
6. Do your jeans have rivets? Do you think rivets are important?
7. Today jeans are very stylish and they change from year to year. What kinds of jeans are in style today? Would you wear jeans that are out of style?
8. Stone-washed jeans, acid-washed jeans, and ragged jeans are made to look as though they are old. What do you think about buying jeans that are not really old but look old? Why do you think these jeans are or were popular?
9. Perhaps there are traditional articles of clothing in your country. What are they? When do you wear them? Do you like to wear them?
10. Do you think it is important to keep your traditional clothing? Why or why not?
11. How can you make sure your traditions are kept and not lost?
12. In the United States, fur coats were once very popular. They were expensive, and having a fur coat was a status symbol that meant you were rich. Now very few people wear fur coats. Do you know why?
13. Are there other fashions that you think are wrong?
14. Have you heard of eco-fashion? Is eco-fashion important for our future?

25. The Nethercutt Museum:
Cars, Cars, and More Cars

15200 Bledsoe Street, Sylmar, CA 91342 (CHECK FOR UPDATES)
Tuesday – Saturday 9:00 A.M. to 4:30 P.M. / Telephone (818) 364-6464. Free.

A city like Florence, Italy, is said to have been **designed** in **proportion** to man. That means a person could walk across the main center of the city in half an hour. Later, cities were designed to be larger to **accommodate** the horse and **carriage**. A horse and carriage could travel across the main center of the city in half an hour. Los Angeles is truly a city designed in proportion to the automobile. By car on the freeway, you can get from one end of the city center to the other in about thirty minutes.

Angelenos love their cars. With the mild weather and little rain, **convertibles** are the perfect choice for anyone who wants to feel the wind and the sun. Another popular type of car is the **hybrid.** There are many on the road today because these cars require little gasoline. The real car lover, however, **goes for** something very rare and unusually beautiful. J.B. and Dorothy Nethercutt were real car lovers. Both died in 2004, but left us a **fascinating** museum. J. B. Netherutt said, "The **recognition** and **preservation** of beauty has been a major focus of my life. It would **suit** me well if what people remembered about me was, 'Where he went, he left beauty behind.'"

1951 ROLLS ROYCE PHANTOM IV

In 1956, at the age of 43, J.B. bought his first two **classic** cars: a 1930 DuPont Town Car and a 1936 Duesenberg Convertible. He spent the next eighteen months (and $65,000) repairing the Du Pont Town Car. His work paid off. In 1958, he won "Best in Show" at Pebble Beach Concours d'Elegance. By 1992 he had won more "Best in Show" awards than anyone else.

In 1971, J.B. and Dorothy opened a museum so that they could **share** these **magnificent** cars with the **public**. An **amazing** car in their collection is the Rolls Royce Phantom IV. It was once owned by Abdullah III Al-Salim Al-Sabah, the last Sheikh (and the first Emir) of Kuwait. Only eighteen of these cars were built.

There are more than 130 cars in the museum, including a 1956 model of the car on the right.

MERCEDES-BENZ 300SL GULLWING COUPE

For those who are not interested in cars, a **guided** tour will let you visit other rooms which have collections including antique dolls, nickelodeons, music boxes, and coins. Outside you can see a 1912 Pullman railcar and a 1937 railroad locomotive. Call to ask about the guided tours.

Those who want to see even more cars can visit the Petersen Automotive Museum at 6060 Wilshire Boulevard Los Angeles, CA 90036 (Telephone 323-930-2277) near the La Brea Tar Pits.

VOCABULARY: MATCHING - MATCH WITHIN THE SAME COLOR

1. _____ to design
2. _____ proportion
3. _____ to accommodate
4. _____ carriage
5. _____ convertible
6. _____ hybrid
7. _____ to go for
8. _____ fascinating
9. _____ recognition
10. _____ preservation
11. _____ to suit
12. _____ classic
13. _____ to share
14. _____ magnificent
15. _____ public
16. _____ amazing
17. _____ gull
18. _____ to guide; guided

A. half and half, such as an electric/gasoline car
B. able to be changed, like a car with/without roof
C. what is pulled by a horse where people can sit
D. to create or plan for a purpose
E. the correct size in relation to other things
F. to have enough space or services for
G. understanding; also, realizing you know
H. keeping something from changing to be like new
I. very interesting
J. very good and has been popular for a long time
K. to really like, or try to get
L. to be right for a person or condition
M. surprisingly good
N. all people
O. to use or own with others or another person
P. big, beautiful, and very impressive
Q. to show places to tourists; shown to tourists
R. a white and gray bird that lives near the sea

DISCUSSION AND CRITICAL THINKING

1. What kinds of cars do you like and why?
2. What kinds of cars should we have in the future? What do you think about hybrid cars?
3. In your opinion, how large is an ideal city and how should people travel in it?
4. Mr. Nethercutt worked in the cosmetics industry. He focused on beauty in all parts of his life. He said, "The recognition and preservation of beauty has been a major focus of my life. It would suit me well if what people remembered about me was, 'Where he went, he left beauty behind.'"
    a. Do you think it takes a special kind of person to recognize beauty? Do you see ugly things around you? If so, why do you think there are these ugly things? Should we do anything about them?
    b. Do you think it is important to care about and preserve beauty? What needs to be preserved?
    c. Mr. Nethercutt wanted to be remembered for leaving beauty in the world. What do you want to be remembered for?

26. The Farmers Market in Los Angeles

What is American food? Chances are you have been eating American food all of your lives. **Tomatoes, potatoes, sweet potatoes, yams, corn, squash, zucchini, sweet peppers, hot peppers, kidney beans, string beans, peanuts, papayas, sunflowers,** and **pineapples** are only some of the fruits, vegetables, and foods that were discovered along with America. Throughout the centuries, these foods have found their way into other countries.

You might have noticed that the tomatoes you get in supermarkets are not as tasty as those you can buy in your country. Most tomatoes in U.S. supermarkets are varieties created especially for marketing: They are beautiful and they last a long time on a supermarket shelf. Unfortunately, they don't have much flavor. If you would like more delicious fruits and vegetables, it is time to take a trip to a farmers' market.

The oldest farmers' market in the area was opened in 1934 on Third Street and Fairfax Avenue in Los Angeles. At that time, the owner of the property, Earl Bell Gilmore, was head of a huge oil company started by his father, Arthur Freemont Gilmore, who discovered oil when he was drilling for water on his dairy farm. E. B. Gilmore had a gift for business: He opened the first self-serve gas stations. To make the experience even more enjoyable, beautiful young women on roller skates would pump gas for those who wanted help.

Even though E. B. Gilmore was a business genius, the idea for the farmers' market was not his. Roger Dahlhjelm and Fred Beck convinced him to let them start the market on his land. Immediately it was a great success as a market, meeting place, and neighborhood center. According to *The Los Angeles Times,* the Farmers Market (no apostrophe) is the best place to see movie stars. Serving customers from all over the world, different market employees speak more than twenty languages. "Meet me at Third and Fairfax" has been used as an invitation for many years in Los Angeles.

FUNNEL

There are other farmers' markets throughout Los Angeles that usually come to a neighborhood once a week. Maybe there is one in your neighborhood. Some farmers' markets have funnel cakes which are made by pouring cake batter through a funnel into hot oil. You might also find some souvenirs among the many crafts sold.

FUNNEL CAKE

A new shopping area next to the Farmers Market is the Grove. Fountains, wonderful shops, and narrow streets closed to traffic give it a European feel. A trolley car made to look like an old Red Car from the Los Angeles electric car and rail system (1874-1961) will take you from the Farmers Market to the Grove and back.

A FOUNTAIN AT THE GROVE

Photo by Bobak Ha'Eri

MATCH THE PICTURES WITH THE WORDS

A.

B.

C.

D.

E.

F.

G.

H.

I.

J.

K.

L.

M.

N.

1. _____ a tomato

2. _____ a potato

3. _____ a yam

4. _____ corn

5. _____ squash

6. _____ zucchini

7. _____ a sweet pepper

8. _____ a hot pepper

9. _____ kidney beans

10. _____ string beans

11. _____ peanuts

12. _____ a sunflower

13. _____ a pineapple

14. _____ a papaya

27. Exploring the Streets of LA

DOLORES DEL RIO, HUDSON AVENUE AT 6529 HOLLYWOOD BOULEVARD
PAINTED BY ALFREDO DE BATUC AND ASSISTANTS
ARUTYUN ARUTYUNIAN, JOHANNA COLEMAN, ARLEN GUTIERREZ, AND JAMES STUBBS

Art can be enjoyed every day in Los Angeles because there are so many murals in the streets. Murals are paintings on walls. Look for them in your neighborhood or visit *publicartinla.com* to find other murals. When you visit the Hollywood Walk of Fame to look at the stars' handprints and footprints in front of TCL Grauman's Chinese Theatre, don't forget to visit Hudson Avenue to see the beautiful mural of Delores Del Rio, a Mexican actress who first became famous in silent films in the United States and continued to act until 1978. She even played Elvis Presley's mother in the movie *Flaming Star* in 1960.

On Lemoyne Street at Sunset Boulevard there is *Quinceanera,* which is a painting of the traditional Mexican birthday party for a 15-year-old girl. This celebrates the day that a girl becomes an adult. One block away at Sunset Boulevard and Echo Park Avenue is *Sculpting Another Destiny*.

QUINCEANERA, LEMOYNE STREET AT SUNSET BOULEVARD
PAINTED BY TERESA POWERS
ASSISTED BY CAROLINA FLORES

SCULPTING ANOTHER DESTINY, SUNSET BOULEVARD AT ECHO PARK AVENUE
PAINTED BY RICARDO MENDOZA AND ASSISTANTS

Photo by Emmalee Garcia   UNION STATION: OUTSIDE

You can also go on a walking tour of your neighborhood or another area of Los Angeles. There are so many interesting sights within walking distance downtown. You can start in Chinatown, walk to Olvera Street, and then visit the train station, Union Station, which was built in 1939. It has beautiful marble floors, flowers, and fountains in courtyards. It is quieter than most stations because there is cork on the walls to absorb noise. From there you can walk to Little Tokyo.

When you get tired of walking, go to the Westin Bonaventure Hotel. Many movies were filmed in this beautiful place. You can see the city as you travel up the glass elevators. The BonaVista Lounge is on the 34th floor. Order a drink or a coffee and just sit as the floor moves to give you a 360 degree view of Los Angeles. On clear days, you can even see the ocean.

AND INSIDE   Photo by Mackerm

Photo by Buchanan-Hermit

CHINATOWN

Photo by Toksave

LITTLE TOKYO

Photo by Geographer

THE WESTIN BONAVENTURE

Photo by Andreas Prefcke

LA CATHEDRAL

Photo by Jon Sullivan

DISNEY CONCERT HALL

Photo by Carol M. Highsmith

TCL GRAUMAN'S CHINESE THEATRE

DISCUSSION AND CRITICAL THINKING

1. By accident, actress Norma Talmadge stepped into wet cement in front of the Chinese Theatre. Sid Grauman decided it was a good idea, and got other actors to put their hands and feet in cement. Can you think of any other happy accidents? Do you think accidents play a part in creativity?
2. Do you like old or new architecture? What is the most beautiful building you have ever seen? Why?
3. In your opinion, what is more important: the inside of a building or the outside of a building?
4. Have you seen any murals in Los Angeles? What is your favorite mural? What do you like about it? What does it make you feel? What kinds of murals do you like?
5. What does *Sculpting Another Destiny* mean? How can a person do that?
6. Graffiti* are messages written by anyone on public walls. It is illegal to write on public walls unless you have special permission. There is a long history of graffiti in Los Angeles, starting in the 1930s. In the early 1980s in Los Angeles, gangs of "writers" started painting graffiti with spray cans and some developed distinctive styles. Some "writers" and graffiti gangs became famous for their styles. A "tag" is just the painted name of a "writer" (a graffiti artist) or a graffiti gang. "Pieces" are more like artwork. Some have pictures, and others just have words. Graffiti "writers" risk prison or trouble with the law. Why do you think they risk so much to put up graffiti?
7. Do you think graffiti are as beautiful as murals? Explain.
8. Graffiti "writers" want to paint, and they want people to see their work. Can you think of another way that these young people can reach this goal?

GRAFFITI IN LOS ANGELES   Photo by A Syn from California

*graffito = singular
graffiti = plural

FOCUS ON PREPOSITIONS

- **Chen:** I'd like to go **to** the BonaVista Lounge to have a drink and just sit for a while.
- **Maria:** The BonaVista Lounge? Is that **in** Hollywood?
- **Chen:** No. It's **downtown**, in the Westin Bonaventure Hotel, **on** Figueroa Street. To be exact, it's **at** 404 Figueroa Street.
- **Maria:** But we won't have time. We have to meet Susan **at** Union Station. Her train is going to arrive **at** five o'clock. Maybe we can take Susan to the BonaVista **in the** evening.
- **Chen:** We'll get a better view of the city **during the** day.
- **Maria:** So let's go tomorrow.
- **Chen:** We're going **to** the Getty Center tomorrow. Maybe we can go **on** Wednesday.
- **Maria:** Wednesday? My parents are going to arrive **in** LA **on** Wednesday. I'm going to meet them **at** the airport.
- **Chen:** Aren't they coming **in** May?
- **Maria:** They are! By Wednesday we will be **in** May!

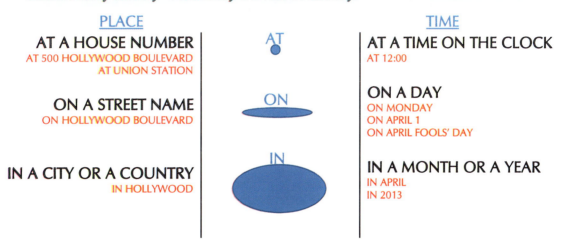

	PLACE		TIME
AT	AT A HOUSE NUMBER AT 500 HOLLYWOOD BOULEVARD AT UNION STATION		AT A TIME ON THE CLOCK AT 12:00
ON	ON A STREET NAME ON HOLLYWOOD BOULEVARD		ON A DAY ON MONDAY ON APRIL 1 ON APRIL FOOLS' DAY
IN	IN A CITY OR A COUNTRY IN HOLLYWOOD		IN A MONTH OR A YEAR IN APRIL IN 2013

ARRIVE **AT** A PLACE ARRIVE **IN** A CITY ARRIVE AT THE AIRPORT ARRIVE IN LOS ANGELES	GO **TO** A PLACE EXCEPT: GO HOME DO NOT USE "TO" WITH DIRECTIONS GO UP/GO DOWN/GO DOWNTOWN GO UPSTAIRS/GO DOWNSTAIRS GO NORTH/GO SOUTH GO EAST/ GO WEST	IN THE MORNING IN THE AFTERNOON IN THE EVENING AT NIGHT DURING THE DAY

	A CAR A TAXI A HELICOPTER (YOU HAVE TO BEND DOWN)	A BUS, A MOTORCYCLE, A BICYCLE, A TRAIN, A HORSE, AN AIRPLANE (YOU DON'T HAVE TO BEND DOWN)
ENTER	GET IN / GET INTO	GET ON
EXIT	GET OUT (OF THE CAR)	GET OFF

Fill in the blanks with the correct preposition or nothing (—):

1. I'm planning to take a vacation ____ September.
2. My vacation starts ____ September 14.
3. Let's go ____ downtown. We can get ____ the bus ____ Wilshire Boulevard.
4. We can take the Vermont Boulevard bus and get ____ ____ Exposition Park.
5. I graduated ____ 2010.
6. I saw Maria getting ____ a taxi on Sunset Boulevard.
7. When you go to the Roosevelt Hotel, be sure to go ____ upstairs to see all the old photographs of Hollywood stars.
8. I'm planning to go ____ home ____ January.
9. My friend is going to arrive ____ the airport ____ 6:00 P.M. ____ Friday.
10. I arrived ____ Los Angeles ____ 2012.
11. It's easy to go ____ San Diego. Just get ____ a train ____ Union Station.
12. Many Americans go on a picnic ____ the 4th of July.
13. ____ Saturdays, I usually get up ____ 9:00 ____ the morning.
14. I like to go sightseeing ____ the day. ____ the evenings I'm usually too tired to go out.
15. I can't stay out late ____ night because I have to get up early ____ the morning.
16. Frank Lloyd Wright designed the Hollyhock House ____ 1917. It is ____ 4800 Hollywood Boulevard ____ Los Angeles.
17. The Hollywood Wax Museum ____ Hollywood Boulevard opened ____ 1965.
18. Your appointment is ____ 2:00 P.M. ____ October 10.
19. The Golden Gate Bridge is ____ San Francisco. If you want to see it, you have to go ____ north.
20. California became the 31st state ____ 1850.

28. Fast Food: McDonald's and Burger King

- **Maria:** Where should we eat lunch?
- **Susan:** There's a fast food restaurant on the corner. We can have a hamburger.
- **Chen:** I like burgers, but I hate mayonnaise, and they sometimes put mayonnaise on burgers.
- **Susan:** Ask them to hold the mayonnaise.
- **Chen:** Hold it?
- **Susan:** Yes. That means you don't want them to give you any mayonnaise.
- **Maria:** I don't want a hamburger. I'm **on a diet**. Fast food is **fattening**.
- **Susan:** You can get salad in some fast food restaurants. Just remember to ask them to hold the salad dressing. Salad dressing can be very fattening. Ask for lemon juice or vinegar. Also, don't buy soda. Get water instead. That's what I do.
- **Chen:** I always carry my own water in a **stainless steel reusable** bottle.
- **Maria:** Why not buy water in a plastic bottle? It's more **convenient**.
- **Chen:** Plastic is bad for the **environment.**

America is known for fast food, perhaps because of our lifestyle with short lunch breaks. As technology creates more possibilities, more is required of us. Worldwide, the **pace** of life is getting faster and faster. Sometimes people have to eat fast food. The key is knowing exactly what you are eating. A new **federal** law has made this easier.

A BURGER AND CURLY FRIES (FRENCH FRIES)

Calories and **nutritional** facts need to be posted in restaurants and on vending machines. In addition, fast food charts with calories and **nutritional** information are **available** at the websites of all the big fast food chains. You can check mcdonalds.com (for McDonald's) and bk.com (for Burger King). You can use their charts to check for sodium (salt), cholesterol, and calories.

A healthy diet includes lots of fruits and vegetables. People should eat from five to thirteen **servings** of fruits and vegetables a day, which is about two and a half cups to six and a half cups a day. The more calories a person needs, the more fruits and vegetables a person should eat. French fries don't count as a vegetable! Potatoes are **carbohydrates**, like bread and rice.

In order to stay healthy, we also have to take care of our **environment**. Plastic can be a problem for our health and for our environment. Fewer than two of every ten plastic bottles are recycled. Much of our plastic ends up in the ocean. The largest area of garbage in the world is in the ocean in a place called the North Pacific Gyre, and it is not far from California. In the ocean, there are six times as many pieces of plastic as there are fish and sea animals. Fish eat plastic, and we eat fish. Every year, plastic kills more than 100,000 sea animals and 1,000,000 seabirds.

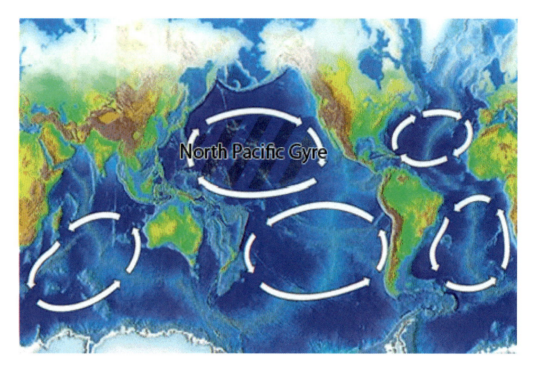

DISCUSSION AND CRITICAL THINKING

The most common **diet** we hear about is a diet to lose weight. However, there are diets to **gain weight**, diets for athletes, low sodium (low salt) diets, and low sugar diets.

Photo by Gila Brand

- Do you see any fruits and vegetables in the photo on the previous page?
- A healthy diet includes five to thirteen **servings** of fruits and vegetables a day. How many servings of fruits and vegetables have you gotten today? Think of some easy ways to eat more fruits and vegetables even if you have a busy **schedule**. Share these ideas with your classmates.
- If you want to **gain weight**, what should you eat? What shouldn't you eat?
- If you want to **lose weight**, what should you eat? What shouldn't you eat?
- If you want to **avoid** (not eat) salt, what should you eat? What shouldn't you eat?
- If you want to **avoid** (not eat) sugar, what should you eat? What shouldn't you eat?

- Have you ever **trained as an athlete**, or do you know anyone who has? Share **details** about an athlete's diet with your classmates.

Most plastic is not **recycled**, and not all plastic can be recycled. Think about all the plastic that you use every day.
- How can you stop using plastic in your life?
- Can you think of ways that businesses can stop using so much plastic?
- What changes will have to be made in the world if we want to stop using so much plastic?

Extra: Web Exploration

1. Let's compare a hamburger from McDonald's to a flame-broiled hamburger from Burger King. Check the websites for information on nutrition.
   a. Which hamburger has fewer calories?
   b. Which hamburger would be better for those who need less sodium?
   c. Which hamburger would be better for those who need less cholesterol?
2. Now let's compare the various Burger King flame-broiled hamburgers.
   a. How many calories does cheese add to the total number of calories?
   b. Which is the hamburger with the most calories?
   c. Which is the hamburger with the most cholesterol?
3. Look at the numbers for the Big Mac and the Whopper.
   a. Check the calories for each. How many calories does the cheese add?
   b. How many calories does the sauce or mayonnaise add?

VOCABULARY: MATCHING - MATCH WITHIN THE SAME COLOR

1. _____ diet (to be/go on a diet)
2. _____ fattening
3. _____ stainless steel
4. _____ reusable
5. _____ convenient
6. _____ environment
7. _____ pace
8. _____ federal
9. _____ nutritional
10. _____ available
11. _____ serving
12. _____ carbohydrate
13. _____ schedule
14. _____ to gain weight
15. _____ to lose weight
16. _____ to avoid
17. _____ to train as an athlete
18. _____ detail
19. _____ to recycle

A. a metal that does not rust (turn orange)
B. making you fat
C. the air, land, and water around where we live
D. easy to use
E. can be used again
F. food one eats as a habit
G. a type of plant for food, like rice or wheat
H. ready to have, buy, or use
I. of the central government, not of the states
J. a normal amount of food to eat at a meal
K. a certain speed
L. about important parts or qualities of food
M. to use old material again
N. to stay away from
O. a small part
P. to seriously practice sports
Q. to take away pounds/kilograms from our body
R. to add pounds or kilograms to our body
S. a plan of time for events, jobs, and duties

29. Chili's Bar and Grill: Another American Restaurant

Photo by Billy Hathorn

This is a restaurant which serves Tex-Mex American food, the Americanized tradition of Mexican food in Texas. The history of Texas is similar to that of California: First there were the Native Americans, then the Spanish. When Mexico won its independence in 1821, Texas became part of Mexico. In 1945, Texas became the 28th state of the United States.

The story of Chili's starts in Terlingua, Texas, where a man named Larry Lavine attended his father-in-law's cook-off in 1967. His father-in-law was the famous car designer and racer, Carroll Shelby. A cook-off is an outdoor cooking competition where people gather to **show off** their special recipes. They cook and sell their own food, usually chili and barbecued ribs. Larry Lavine **discovered** that he really loved cook-offs, and he wanted to share his love with others.

Although there are now over 1,400 Chili's restaurants worldwide, the first restaurant was opened in 1975 by Larry Lavine in an old postal station in Dallas, Texas. His plan was to serve great food in a casual **environment**. Today, every Chili's restaurant keeps the casual style. When you go to Chili's, look around the restaurant. Check the **tiles** on the floor for dog **footprints**. Also, according to tradition, one photo in the restaurant is hung upside down. Chili's is famous for gourmet burgers, ribs, and grilled food, including a Tex-Mex favorite called fajitas.

According to Frank Patterson, a Texan who **witnessed** the creation of this dish, fajitas were first made by a Mexican cowboy from the Chapparosa Ranch outside Del Rio, Texas. In the 1960s, cowboys were paid only $5 per day along with **room and board**. Of course, a smart employer would serve the cheapest food possible. When hamburger meat started rising in price (from $0.29 to $0.69 per pound), the head cowboy at the ranch saw that the butcher would cut off the strap muscle of the cow's belly (a tough meat with tendons) and sell it for only $0.10 a pound as dog food. He started buying this meat for his cowboys. He learned that if he grilled it and cut it across the grain, it was quite good. A few years later, he started selling his specialty at a local festival called Bergesfest. He attracted the attention of a local businessman and together they opened their own restaurant in San Antonio, Texas, called "Taco Cabana."

In 1976, Larry Lavine opened a second Chili's restaurant. At that time, fajitas were not on the menu. They served chili (a stew with meat, beans, tomatoes and hot red chili peppers), burgers, tacos, and homemade fries—in baskets, not on plates. By 1983, there were already twenty-three Chili's restaurants! Norman Brinker bought these restaurants and turned them into the international chain we know today. In 1984, they started serving fajitas for the first time and had to start using plates.

Like all restaurants today, Chili's provides nutrition and **allergy** information. If you are **allergic** or **intolerant** to certain foods, you can look on the Internet to see which dishes are right for you. You can also plan your menu or even order online. You might be surprised to learn that some of the **items** on the menu have more than 2,000 calories, which is considered the normal amount that a person should eat in an entire day. A healthy menu is one that you plan carefully.

CHILI PEPPERS

VOCABULARY: MATCHING - MATCH WITHIN THE SAME COLOR

1. _____ to show off
2. _____ to discover
3. _____ environment
4. _____ tile
5. _____ footprint
6. _____ to witness
7. _____ room and board
8. _____ allergy
9. _____ allergic
10. _____ intolerant
11. _____ item

A. the impression or mark left by a foot
B. the air, land and water around where we live
C. baked clay for covering floors, roofs, or walls
D. to find something that was not known before
E. to try to make people think you are great
F. extreme sensitivity to foods, etc. causing sickness
G. a thing
H. a place to sleep and food to eat
I. your body will not digest (accept) certain foods
J. extremely sensitive to food--a person gets very sick
K. to see something as it happens

Ordering in a Restaurant

- **Waiter:** What would you like?
- **Abdullah:** Beef fajitas.
- **Waiter:** Would you like tortillas and condiments with that?
- **Abdullah:** Yes, please.
- **Waiter:** Can I get you anything to drink?
- **Abdullah:** Just water.
  (To Dong)
- **Waiter:** And what would you like?
- **Dong:** A burger.
- **Waiter:** What kind?
- **Dong:** I guess I'll have to look at the menu.

Practice **ordering** in a restaurant with your partner. One of you will take the role of the waiter; the other will take the role of the customer. Then change roles.

DISCUSSION AND CRITICAL THINKING

1. We studied the word "intolerant" in the chapter on Gene Autry. We can use this word in different ways. What does "intolerant" mean in this chapter? Do you remember what "intolerant" means in the chapter on Gene Autry?
2. If you are intolerant or allergic to a type of food, what should you do? What should you ask in a restaurant?
3. The recipe for fajitas was created because the cowboys in Texas needed cheap food. We have the saying, "Necessity is the mother of invention." Can you think of other things that were invented because someone needed something?
4. What do we need in the world today? Would you like to create something that we need? If so, what is it?

Extra: Web Exploration

Consider these common items on a menu at Chili's:

an avocado burger	a chicken Caesar salad	grilled salmon
a country-fried steak	the house salad	baby back ribs
a sirloin steak	a grilled chicken salad	cheesecake
a Caribbean salad	fried shrimp	a burger

1. Look at Chili's menu. What are "condiments"? Can you guess?
2. For a person on a diet, what would you recommend at Chili's?
3. Chili's is famous for the Big Mouth burger. How many calories are in it? Which menu items have even more calories?
4. Which item has the least amount of salt?
5. Why is there so much fat, and why is there so much salt in these menu items?
6. According to the U.S. government, a person with the average 2,000-calorie-per-day diet should have not more than 20 grams of saturated fat and 65 grams of total fat per day. Which menu items fulfill this requirement?
7. According to the U.S. government, a person with the average 2,000-calorie-per-day diet should have not more than 2400 milligrams of sodium (salt) per day. Which menu items fulfill this requirement?
8. According to the U.S. government, a person with the average 2,000-calorie-per-day diet should have at least 300 grams of carbohydrates per day. Which menu items fulfill this requirement?
9. According to the U.S. government, a person with the average 2,000-calorie-per-day diet should have at least 25 grams of fiber per day. Which menu items fulfill this requirement?
10. What do you plan on eating at Chili's?

30. Starbucks

CAPPUCCINO

This is not simply a coffee shop. Although there are 17,000 Starbucks worldwide, this is not only a business. Starbucks has a **mission**: "To **inspire** and **nurture** the human spirit – one person, one cup and one neighborhood at a time." This gives new meaning to the words, "coffee break." Starbucks wants to **provide** an **environment** that is completely different from our everyday problem-filled world.

An English teacher (Jerry Baldwin), a history teacher (Zev Siegl), and a writer (Gordon Bowker) **founded** the company in Seattle in 1970. They named it after the character Starbucks from the American novel by Herman Melville, *Moby Dick*. Originally, they did not sell drinks. They roasted coffee beans and provided only the beans to customers. In 1982, Howard Schultz became part of the company. After a trip to Italy, he was inspired to sell coffee as they do in Italy. In the 1990s, the company started to set up stores in other cities.

Besides providing customers with a wonderful experience, the company is also very **conscientious**. They make sure that their coffee is grown in a **sustainable** way so that water is not wasted and not many chemicals are used in farming. They make sure that all workers, including the farmers, are paid enough.

They want their stores to have a very small environmental **footprint,** which means they use as little energy, water, and as few things from the environment as possible. They are changing all their light bulbs to LED bulbs (light-emitting diodes). These bulbs use a little more than 1/9 as much electricity as the old **incandescent** bulbs since a 7-watt LED bulb can give as much light as a 60-watt incandescent bulb. These bulbs use even less than compact fluorescent bulbs (CFB) which use 13-15 watts to give as much light as a 60-watt incandescent bulb.

Only paints low in volatile organic compounds (VOC) are used in Starbucks stores because bad paint can harm our health and the environment. In fact, all their new buildings will be certified by LEED (Leadership in Energy and Environmental Design).

Since many of the coffee drinks were inspired by the Italian coffee tradition, it will help you to understand some Italian to order:
- caffè = coffee
- espresso = express (more quickly than usual); a way of making coffee quickly and especially for the customer by using a special coffee machine
- latte = milk
- caffè latte = coffee with milk
- macchiato = spotted, with a spot, or stained
- caffè macchiato = coffee with a little (a spot) of milk
- latte macchiato = milk with a little (a spot) of coffee
- cappuccino = coffee with milk in it. This is named after the dark brown color of the clothing worn by the Capuchin monks. In fact, cappuccino has proportionally more coffee in it than caffè latte (Starbucks adds more milk to its caffè latte), and very much more milk than is in caffè macchiato. In addition, the milk in cappuccino is foamed on top.

Other words you may need at Starbucks:

CINNAMON

- cinnamon = a reddish-brown spice from tree bark

- frappuccino = a Starbucks drink made of ice, coffee, and milk

- hazelnut =

- mocha = a drink made with coffee and chocolate

- nutmeg = a brown spice that is grated from something that looks like an oval nut

NUTMEG

INCANDESCENT LIGHT BULB
OLD

COMPACT FLUORESCENT
LIGHT BULB
NEWER

LED LIGHT BULB
THE NEWEST

Secret Menus

If you really want to be cool, you can order something that is not on the menu. If you ask for a Zebra Mocha (also called a Tuxedo Mocha), you will get a mocha made with half regular chocolate and half white chocolate. A Captain Crunch is a strawberries and cream frappuccino with caramel (sugar heated and browned), hazelnut flavor, toffee (candy made with sugar and butter), and chocolate chips. Study Starbucks' secret menu on the Internet. Most of the time you will get what you ask for, but sometimes the person serving you doesn't know what you are talking about. After all, the menu is secret! If that happens, just explain what you want. You can have even more fun by combining items on the menu to create your own special drinks.

ZEBRA

STRAWBERRY

TUXEDO

READING COMPREHENSION

1. What is the mission of Starbucks?
2. Who founded the company and when did they found it?
3. What did they do before they started Starbucks?
4. Why did they name their company Starbucks?
5. Who joined the company in 1982? What did he do?
6. Why is Starbucks considered a conscientious company?
7. What has Starbucks done to make a smaller environmental footprint?
8. Where can you find information about Starbucks' secret menu?

VOCABULARY: MATCHING - MATCH WITHIN THE SAME COLOR

1. _____ mission
2. _____ to inspire
3. _____ to nurture
4. _____ to provide
5. _____ environment
6. _____ to found
7. _____ conscientious
8. _____ sustainable
9. _____ footprint
10. _____ incandescent
11. _____ spice

A. the air, land and water around where we live
B. to take care of and help grow
C. to give or supply
D. a goal, important job, or duty
E. to help someone get an idea, or encourage
F. the impression or mark left by a foot
G. keeping a balance without using up all resources
H. producing light when hot
I. to start a town or a company
J. careful to do everything right
K. part of a plant (not the leaf) used to flavor food

DISCUSSION AND CRITICAL THINKING

1. What do you think about the mission of Starbucks?
2. Do you have a mission in life? Do you want to have a mission in life?
3. Have you thought about the footprint you leave in the world (often called the carbon footprint)?
4. What are some small changes that you can make so that you will leave a smaller footprint?
5. Think about the business plan of Starbucks. What are they really selling (not coffee)? Is this a good marketing plan? Why or why not?

31. A Change in Diet

In coming to the U.S., you changed your diet. Any change in diet can create digestive problems. A common problem is lactose intolerance. Lactose is a milk sugar. The lactase enzyme breaks down the lactose so it can be digested. Many people lose the ability to digest milk and milk products as they grow up. This is not an allergy, but may cause digestive problems such as nausea (stomach problems), diarrhea (running to the toilet all the time), gas, pain, and bloating (your abdomen gets bigger like a balloon).

Look at the map below. Find your country and the percentage of people who have lactose intolerance. This is usually common in countries that traditionally do not eat cheese or dairy (milk) products. Check out the United States. The rate of lactose intolerance is similar to England and Northern Europe. You will also find that Americans put milk and cheese in almost everything. If you find you have a problem with dairy products, just say, "Hold the cheese."

OBSERVE YOUR HEALTH

1. Do you have more headaches than usual? Some people start drinking more coffee and caffeinated colas than they did at home. This can cause headaches in some people. A constant amount of coffee may be okay, but one cup too many or one cup too few may give you headaches.
2. Other common foods that cause intolerance are: sugar, corn, wheat, soy, yeast (used in bread and beer), and eggs. Are you eating more or less of these foods than you did at home?

The Percentage of Lactose Intolerance Around the World
Map by Rainer Zenz

VOCABULARY REVIEW PUZZLE #2

ACROSS
1. the study of knowledge, life, and what is good or bad
2. not accepting of anything different
4. to tell someone a secret
6. all people
7. what you must do legally, or morally (to be good); responsibility
10. money that you owe (have to pay back to someone)
12. to get by looking for
13. to grow into an adult
14. in nature, without control by people
17. a person who goes into another country to live
20. to begin to live in a place
21. illness caused by eating something that can kill
22. the air, land and water around where we live
24. someone who has the job of protecting others
25. the person who starts a town, business, or organization
27. after being trapped, allow to be free
28. someone who goes to another place to find work

DOWN
1. to say something is against the law or not allowed
3. a general feeling
5. show
8. a belief in the honesty of someone
9. to create or plan for a purpose
11. not existing anymore
15. to damage completely
16. very interesting
18. easy to have, buy, or use
19. in a dangerous situation; it might soon be extinct
21. to have or own
23. something that is grown or made or sold
26. a long serious talk, usually to a group

HINTS

A list of the words for the crossword puzzle on the previous page.

available
confide
debt
design
destroy
duty
endangered
environment
exhibit
extinct
fascinating
find
founder
guard
immigrant
intolerant
lecture
mature
migrant
mood
philosophy
poisoning
possess
product
prohibit
public
release
settle
trust
wild

Vocabulary Index

The following is a list of the words focused on in this text along with the chapter or chapters in which these words appear. Check the table of contents to get the page number of the chapter. * = this word is on Averil Coxhead's Academic Word List.

A
*abandon (Leonis Adobe)
*accommodate (The Nethercutt)
acorn (The First People)
acrylic painting (The Getty)
adoption (Iroquois League; Orcutt Ranch; Puzzle #1)
advantage (Leonis Adobe)
agriculture (S.F. Mission)
agricultural (El Pueblo)
allergic (Chili's)
allergy (Chili's)
allow (Leonis Adobe; Puzzle #1)
altar (S.F. Mission)
amazing (The Nethercutt)
amphitheater (Griffith Observatory)
ancient (The Getty)
anemone (The Beaches)
angel (El Pueblo)
antiquity (The Getty)
approval (Iroquois League; Puzzle #1)
approve (Iroquois League)
architect (The Getty)
arm (Leonis Adobe)
arrest (Obligations)
artifact (Gene Autry)
asphalt (La Brea Tar Pits; The First People; Puzzle #1)
*available (Fast Food; Griffith Observatory; Puzzle #2)
avoid (Fast Food)
awesome (LA Zoo)

B
ban (LA Zoo)
bakery (Getting Around)
bargain (El Pueblo)
basket (The First People; Gene Autry)
bead (The First People)
beans (S.F. Mission)
beauty salon (Getting Around)
bison (La Brea Tar Pits)
bookstore (Getting Around)
breed (LA Zoo)
brick (El Pueblo)
bullets (LA Zoo)

C
café (Getting Around)
cage (LA Zoo)
camel (La Brea Tar Pits)
candle (El Pueblo)
capture (LA Zoo)
carbohydrate (Fast Food)
carriage (The Nethercutt)
carve (S.F. Mission)
cattle (S.F. Mission)
ceramics (The Getty)
cinnamon (Starbucks)
claim (The First People; Leonis Adobe; Puzzle #1)
classic (The Nethercutt)
collar (Obligations)
colony (Iroquois League)
commercially (La Brea Tar Pits; Puzzle #1)
commissioner (Iroquois League)
*commit suicide (Leonis Adobe)
compact fluorescent light bulb or CFL (Starbucks)
*compensation (The First People; Puzzle #1)
confide (Gene Autry; Puzzle #2)
conscientious (Starbucks)
conserve (LA Zoo)
*constitution (Iroquois League)
*consultant (The Getty)
*contract (Leonis Adobe)
*contribution (El Pueblo)
convenient (Fast Food)

convento (S.F. Mission)
*convert (S.F. Mission)
convertible (The Nethercutt)
copy shop (Getting Around)
corn (The Farmers Market)
cosmopolitan (El Pueblo)
coyote (La Brea Tar Pits; Orcutt Ranch)
custom (Iroquois League)
customer (Blue Jeans)

D

damage (S.F. Mission; Puzzle #1)
debt (Griffith Observatory; Puzzle #2)
defenseless (Leonis Adobe)
dentist (Getting Around)
design (Blue Jeans; The Nethercutt; Puzzle #2)
destroy (Leonis Adobe; Puzzle #1; The Getty; Puzzle #2)
detail (Fast Food)
diet (Fast Food)
dig (S.F. Mission)
dire wolf (La Brea Tar Pits)
disappear (Leonis Adobe)
disappointed (The First People)
discover (S.F. Mission ; Orcutt Ranch; Puzzle #1; Chili's)
dishonor (The First People; Puzzle #1)
distress (Gene Autry)
*diversity (El Pueblo)
dome (Griffith Observatory)
drawings (The Getty)
drypoint (The Getty)
duty (LA Zoo; Griffith Observatory; Puzzle #2)

E

eagle (La Brea)
egg tempera (The Getty)
elderly (Gene Autry)
elementary school (Getting Around)
encaustic (The Getty)
endangered (LA Zoo; Puzzle #2)
endeavor (The Getty)
engravings (The Getty)
enslave (The First People)
entrepreneur (El Pueblo)

*environment (Fast Food; Chili's; LA Zoo; Puzzle #2; Starbucks)
epidemic (The First People)
epoch (La Brea Tar Pits)
*establish (Iroquois League)
etchings (The Getty)
*ethnic (El Pueblo)
Etruria (The Getty)
*exhibit (Gene Autry; Puzzle #2)
expire (Blue Jeans)
explorer (El Pueblo)
extinct (La Brea Tar Pits; Puzzle #1; LA Zoo; Puzzle #2)

F

fabric (Blue Jeans)
*facility (The Beaches)
fascinating (The Beaches; The Nethercutt; Puzzle #2)
fattening (Fast Food)
*federal (Fast Food; Iroquois League)
fiction/fictional (The First People; Puzzle #1)
file a claim (Leonis Adobe)
find / past=found (LA Zoo; The Getty; Puzzle #2)
fine (Obligations)
fitness center (Getting Around)
florist shop (Getting Around)
footprint (Chili's; Starbucks)
foreclosure (Leonis Adobe)
former (El Pueblo)
fossil (La Brea Tar Pits)
fossil fuel (La Brea Tar Pits)
*found (The First People; El Pueblo; Puzzle #1; Starbucks)
*founder (Gene Autry; Puzzle #2)
*founding (Iroquois League)
frappuccino (Starbucks)
freedom (El Pueblo)
furnish (El Pueblo; Leonis Adobe)

G

gain weight (Fast Food)
gas station (Getting Around)
gentle (Gene Autry)
geology (Orcutt Ranch)
get (LA Zoo)

gliclée (The Getty)
glimpse (Leonis Adobe)
go for (The Nethercutt)
goat (Leonis Adobe)
greed (Leonis Adobe; Puzzle #1)
greedy (S.F. Mission)
ground (The Getty)
guard (LA Zoo; Puzzle #2)
guide (The Nethercutt)
gull (The Nethercutt)

H
habitat (LA Zoo)
handicapped (Obligations)
hardware store (Getting Around)
haste (The First People)
hawk (Griffith Observatory)
hazelnut (Starbucks)
heal (La Brea Tar Pits)
heir (Leonis Adobe)
heritage (The First People; Puzzle #1)
hire (Leonis Adobe; Puzzle #1)
hog (S.F. Mission)
hoof (Gene Autry)
horse (La Brea Tar Pits)
hospital (Getting Around)
hot pepper (The Farmers Market)
human (La Brea Tar Pits)
hybrid (The Nethercutt)

I
ice cream shop (Getting Around)
*illegal (Obligations; The First People; El Pueblo; Leonis Adobe; Puzzle #1)
*immigrant (Blue Jeans; Puzzle #2)
incandescent (Starbucks)
independence (El Pueblo)
inherit (Leonis Adobe)
inheritance (Leonis Adobe)
inspire (Starbucks)
intimidate (Leonis Adobe)
intolerant (Gene Autry; Puzzle #2; Chili's)
irrigation (S.F. Mission)
*item (Blue Jeans; Chili's)

J

K
keep track of (LA Zoo)
kidney beans (The Farmers Market)

L
land (El Pueblo)
lasting (The Getty)
laundromat (Getting Around)
lead - noun (LA Zoo)
league (Iroquois League)
leash (Obligations)
leather (El Pueblo)
lecture (The Getty; Puzzle #2)
LED (light emitting diode) (Starbucks)
limitation (The First People)
lithographs (The Getty)
litter (Obligations)
locksmith (Getting Around)
lose weight (Fast Food)

M
magnificent (The Nethercutt)
mammoth (La Brea Tar Pits)
manage (Leonis Adobe; Blue Jeans)
manufacture (Blue Jeans)
marine (La Brea Tar Pits)
material (The First People)
materialistic (Puzzle #1)
*mature (LA Zoo; Puzzle #2)
mayor (El Puelblo)
metal (Blue Jeans)
*migrant (Gene Autry; Puzzle #2)
*minority (El Pueblo)
mirror (Iroquois League)
mission (Starbucks)
mocha (Starbucks)
moderation (The First People)
monogamous (LA Zoo)
monoprint (The Getty)
mood (The Beaches; Puzzle #2)
movie theatre (Getting Around)
museum (Getting Around)

N
novel (The First People)
nurture (Starbucks)
nutmeg (Starbucks)
nutritional (Fast Food)

O
obligation (Griffith Observatory; Obligations)
observatory (Griffith Observatory)

official (S.F. Mission)
oil painting (The Getty)
original (El Pueblo)
owner (El Pueblo)

P
pace (Fast Food)
paintings (The Getty)
papaya (The Farmers Market)
pastels (The Getty)
patent (Blue Jeans)
path (The Beaches)
patriot (Gene Autry)
peanuts (The Farmers Market)
performance (The Getty)
performer (The Beaches)
pet shop (Getting Around)
pharmacy (Getting Around)
*philosophy (The First People; Puzzle #1; Gene Autry; Puzzle #2)
pineapple (The Farmers Market)
pit (La Brea Tar Pits)
pitifully (The Getty)
poisoning (LA Zoo; Puzzle #2)
*policy (Iroquois League)
pool (The Beaches)
possess (Gene Autry; Puzzle #2)
post office (Getting Around)
potato (The Farmers Market)
prehistoric (La Brea Tar Pits)
preservation (The Nethercutt)
preserve (La Brea Tar Pits)
*principle (The First People; Orcutt Ranch; Puzzle #1)
prints (The Getty)
*procedure (Iroquois League)
*process (Iroquois League)
*producer (El Pueblo)
product (The Getty; Puzzle #2)
professional (El Pueblo)
profit (The First People)
*prohibit (The Beaches; Puzzle #2)
property (Leonis Adobe)
*proportion (The Nethercutt)
prosper (Griffith Observatory)
prosperous (S.F. Mission; Leonis Adobe; Puzzle #1)

protect (Blue Jeans)
provide (Starbucks)
public (El Pueblo; The Nethercutt; Puzzle #2)
pulpit (S.F. Mission)
purse (El Pueblo)

Q

R
racially (Gene Autry)
recede (La Brea Tar Pits)
recognition (The Nethercutt)
recognize (The First People; Puzzle #1)
recycle (Fast Food)
redwood (The First People)
*release (LA Zoo; Puzzle #2)
remain (Puzzle #1)
remains (La Brea Tar Pits)
renovate (Leonis Adobe; Puzzle #1)
republic (El Pueblo)
*require (Blue Jeans)
reservation (The First People)
*resource (The First People)
*retain (Iroquois League)
reusable (Fast Food)
rivet (Blue Jeans)
romance (The First People)
room and board (Chili's)

S
saber-toothed cat (La Brea Tar Pits)
salesclerk (El Pueblo)
scavenger (La Brea Tar Pits; Puzzle #1; LA Zoo)
*schedule (Fast Food)
screenprints (The Getty)
sculpture(s) (The Getty)
serving (s) (Fast Food)
settle (Griffith Observatory; Puzzle #2)
settlement (El Pueblo; La Brea Tar Pits; Puzzle #1)
settler (El Pueblo; The First People; Leonis Adobe)
shade (Orcutt Ranch)
share (Blue Jeans)
share (Leonis Adobe; The Nethercutt)
sheep (S.F. Mission)
shell (The First People; The Beaches)

shepherd (Leonis Adobe)
shoe store (Getting Around)
shoot (LA Zoo)
short-faced bear (La Brea)
show off (Chili's)
shrewd (Leonis Adobe)
slave (El Pueblo; The First People; Puzzle #1)
slavery (El Pueblo; Iroquois League)
sloth (La Brea Tar Pits)
smallpox (The First People)
smuggle (Leonis Adobe)
solar (Griffith Observatory)
souvenir (The Beaches; El Pueblo)
span (La Brea Tar Pits; LA Zoo)
spice (Starbucks)
spring (S.F. Mission)
squash (The Farmers Market)
stainless steel (Fast Food)
starfish (The Beaches)
steal (Blue Jeans)
stingy (Leonis Adobe)
string beans (The Farmers Market)
suffer (The First People; Puzzle #1)
suicide (Leonis Adobe)
suit (The Nethercutt)
*sum (Leonis Adobe)
sunbathing (The Beaches)
sunflower (The Farmers Market)
supermarket (Getting Around)
supply (S.F. Mission; Blue Jeans)
surface (La Brea Tar Pits)
sustainable (Starbucks)
sweet pepper (The Farmers Market)

T
tag (Obligations; LA Zoo)
tailor (Blue Jeans)
take advantage (Leonis Adobe; Gene Autry)
tangible (The First People)
tar (La Brea Tar Pits)
taxes (Obligations)
tear (past=torn) (Blue Jeans)
tenant (Leonis Adobe)

thatched (The First People)
tide (The Beaches)
tile (Chili's)
tomato (The Farmers Market)
trail (Griffith Observatory)
train (Fast Food)
trapped (La Brea Tar Pits)
trust (Gene Autry; Puzzle #2)

U
unanimous (Iroquois League)
unified (Iroquois League)

V
veto (Iroquois League)
vine (El Pueblo)

W
walnut (S.F. Mission)
watercolor (The Getty)
wealthy (Leonis Adobe)
weave (The First People)
western horse (La Brea Tar Pits)
wheat (S.F. Mission)
widow (Leonis Adobe)
wild (LA Zoo; Griffith Observatory; Puzzle #2)
window-shop (The Beaches)
wine (El Pueblo)
wine shop (Getting Around)
winery (El Pueblo)
witness (Chili's)
woodcuts (The Getty)

Y
yam (The Farmers Market)
yodel (Gene Autry)

Z
zucchini (The Farmers Market)

Answer Key

Page 3
1. What is your name?
2. What city are you from?
3. What is your telephone number?
4. What is your Skype address?
5. What is your email address?
6. What is your favorite city?
7. What is your favorite city like?

Answers vary. Examples of possible answers:
My name is Chen.
I am from Beijing.
My telephone number is _____.
My Skype address is _____.
My email address is _____.
Rome is my favorite city. It is big, busy, and has many interesting museums and old buildings.

Page 6
Answers vary. Examples of possible answers:
Los Angeles is warmer than my city, and it is more spacious.

Page 10
Tom isn't as tall as Jack.

Page 12
Count nouns: book, pencil, onion, tomato, orange.
1. -----
2. The
3. -----
4. a, The
5. -----
6. The
7. -----
8. The
9. The
10. -----
11. the
12. -----, -----, -----
13. the, -----, -----
14. the, -----, the, -----
15. -----, the, the, -----
16. a
17. a, the, The, the, a, -----
18. -----, the
19. -----, The
20. the, ----, ----, ----, ----, ----
21. -----, the
22. the
23. a
24. the
25. an, a

Page 13
1. hotter
2. more romantic
3. A
4. -----, cheaper, -----
5. the, -----
6. busier
7. exciting
8. cosmopolitan
9. A, a
10. polite
11. bigger
12. more relaxing

13. -----, delicious
14. -----, -----
15. the, the, the
16. -----, sweeter
17. A, friendlier, a
18. -----
19. -----, more convenient
20. A, more interesting, a
21. -----, more important, ----- (We don't count money! We count dollars and cents.)
22. -----, more difficult, -----
23. -----, tastier, -----
24. -----, a, -----
25. -----, worse, -----

Page 18
1. prosperous
2. attractive
3. tall*
4. modern

*narrow things are tall; wide things are high

Page 19
Exercise #1: Circle the correct adjective:
1. a little
2. a few
3. a little
4. a few

Exercise #2: Circle the correct adjective:
1. few
2. a little
3. a few
4. little

Exercise #3: Circle the correct adjective:
1. fewer
2. less
3. fewer
4. less

Exercise #4: Circle the correct adjective:
1. too
2. very

Page 21
(pronunciation only – this is **not** the correct spelling)
1. playd
2. closd
3. drest
4. ended
5. studyd
6. livd
7. likt
8. hated

Page 23
1. most interesting
2. so many
3. too
4. visited
5. a little
6. happy
7. am going to
8. busier
9. will
10. much, less
11. such, so

12. very
13. too
14. went
15. busy
16. most talented
17. talented
18. younger
19. less
20. fewer

Page 27
1. have been
2. have just ordered
3. were
4. Have you ever been
5. have never had
6. visited
7. have lived
8. raised
9. has raised
10. graduated
11. appeared
12. has appeared
13. had
14. was
15. watched
16. have watched

Page 30
1. made
2. sent
3. had
4. seen
5. spoken
6. done
7. seen
8. seen
9. read
10. eaten
11. eaten
12. made
13. spoken
14. shopped
15. asked
16. listened

Page 32
since April
for six minutes
for twelve weeks
since 8:00 A.M.
since September 22nd
since midnight
for five months
since May 21st
since New Year's Day
for one second
since Tuesday
for seven years

1. He has lived in LA since 2000. He has lived in LA for ____ years.
2. He has worked since 2005. He has worked for ____ years.
3. He has studied since 2006. He has studied for ____ years.
4. He has owned a car since 2009. He has owned a car for ____ years.
5. He has had a dog since 2010. He has had a dog for ____ years.

Page 36
1. well
2. beautifully
3. intelligent
4. fast
5. sloppily
6. beautiful
7. beautiful
8. accurately
9. neatly
10. neat
11. carefully
12. carelessly
13. careless

Note: Comparative adverbs are easy. Just add "more." For example: She sings more beautifully than her sister. OR: He translates more accurately than anyone I know.
The **EXCEPTIONS** use "-er." For example: He drives faster than his father. She arrived earlier than the boss. He speaks better than his brother.

Page 38
Example: more interesting
1. difficult
2. for
3. have lived
4. carelessly
5. beautiful
6. comfortable
7. met
8. --
9. The, --
10. recorded
11. most beautiful
12. in (since cannot be used because the action of "met" does not continue into the present)
13. since
14. slowly
15. the, a
16. hard
17. have visited
18. good
19. met
20. has recorded
21. more important
22. lived
23. good
24. accurately
25. the

Page 40
1. She was marketing her perfume.
2. People did not know what caused AIDS and they were very afraid of it.
3. She got people to contribute to HIV/AIDS charities and she got members of Congress to listen to her.
4. She spoke to members of Congress to help pass a law that prevents discrimination against people with HIV.
5. She taught him to be outgoing, understanding, generous, open-minded, and fair.

Page 41
Answers vary. Examples of possible answers:
I was sleeping at 11:00 P.M. I was playing tennis all morning last Saturday.
Review
1. most courageous
2. braver
3. famous
4. best
5. appeared
6. was watching
7. fast
8. the. has lived, for
9. ---, more expensive, ---
10. well

Review question structures:
1. was
2. did
3. is
4. has
5. will

Page 43
Possible answers:
1. He was working when the plane arrived.
2. She was talking on the phone. He was reading the newspaper when the plane arrived.
3. They were having coffee. OR: They were kissing.
4. She was speaking on the phone and using her computer (or using her laptop).
5. They were watching the plane arrive. OR: They were waiting for the plane to arrive.
6. They were walking and talking when the plane arrived.
7. She was telling a secret when the plane arrived.
8. She was sitting on the floor and using her computer.
9. She was texting her husband on her cell phone when the plane arrived.
10. She was running when the plane arrived.
11. He was drinking a beer when the plane arrived.
12. He was writing when the plane arrived.
13. She was buying a ticket when the plane arrived.
14. They were walking and talking.
15. She was talking on her cell phone.
16. They were eating. OR: They were talking.
17. She was eating a hot dog when the plane arrived.
18. He was speaking on his cell phone and using his computer when the plane arrived.
19. She was serving a customer. OR: She was selling fast food when the plane arrived.
20. She was selling a ticket when the plane arrived.

Page 45
1. C
2. D
3. B
4. D
5. C
6. A
7. C
8. D

Page 46
1. What do you eat in the evening?
2. What kind of music do you like?
3. Where do you go dancing?
4. How far did you walk yesterday?
5. Who(m*) did you talk to last night?
6. Where did you stay last week?
7. Where is your friend going?
8. What Internet game are you playing?
9. Who(m*) are you calling?
10. Can you help me carry my luggage?
11. Will it rain tomorrow?
12. Where should I go (if I want to see flowers)?

* Although it is more correct to use "whom" when speaking or writing about the object of a sentence, "who" is often used, especially when speaking.

Page 51-53
Answers vary. Examples of possible answers:
(For letter #1)
You should speak to your roommate OR: You should buy food that your roommate doesn't like. Then she won't eat it. OR: You should buy a small refrigerator for your food and put a lock on it. OR: You should buy a locked box for your food and put it in the refrigerator.

Page 55
1. seen
2. met
3. bought
4. eaten
5. seen
6. watched
7. crashed
8. gotten
9. been
10. spoken
11. stayed
12. stopped
13. danced
14. driven
15. jogged

Page 56
1. before
2. as soon as
3. until
4. while
5. If (or When)
6. After
7. If
8. When

Page 59
A. 7
B. 6

169

C. 2
D. 3
E. 5
F. 4
G. 1

Page 63
Answers vary. Examples of possible answers:
Traffic regulations:
You must stop at a stop sign. You mustn't (or must not) drive too fast.
Family rules:
You must wash the dishes. You mustn't (or must not) play loud music.

Dorm rules:
You must pay the rent. You mustn't (or must not) have a dog.

Page 64
Answers vary. Examples of possible answers:
The policeman or woman answers:
If you drive too fast, I will give you a ticket. OR: If you drive too fast I will give you a fine. OR: If you drive too fast, I will fine you.
You answer the policeman or woman:
If I don't have a collar and name tags on my dog, you will fine me. OR: If I don't have a collar and name tags on my dog, I might lose my dog.

Page 65
Examples of questions with "must."
The answers, or the discussion, vary.
1. If I want to enter an American university, what must I do?
2. If my sister wants to come to Los Angeles, what must she do?
Examples of questions with "have to."
The answers, or the discussion, vary.
1. If I want to learn how to drive, what do I have to do?
2. If my brother wants to take care of his teeth, what does he have to do?

Page 66
1. must not
2. don't have to
3. must not
4. don't have to*
5. don't have to*
6. don't have to*
7. must not
8. must not
9. don't have to
10. must not

* The answers depend on the rules of the school.

Page 67
Answers vary. Examples of possible sentences:
If you want a promotion, you must work hard. OR: If you want a promotion, you have to work hard.
If you want to learn English fast, you must not think in your native language.
If you want a lot of friends, you don't have to be rich or spend a lot of money.

Page 68
Answers vary. Examples of possible sentences:
1. You should go to the library and take out a book.

Page 70
1. make
2. take
3. take
4. make
5. get
6. do
7. make
8. make
9. make
10. get
11. make
12. get
13. do
14. take
15. take
16. get
17. make
18. make
19. Take
20. Make
21. do
22. make
23. make
24. gets
25. gets

Page 71
Answers vary. Examples of possible sentences:
We should take a guitar. If we take a guitar, we will be able to play music. We have to take a book on health care. We must take a knife. We don't have to take a guitar. A book on health care is more important than a guitar. A knife is the most important item. I have always used a knife for protection. I have always used a knife to cut.

Page 75
1. The window was broken by Bob.
2. The cake will be eaten by us.
3. Many notes have been written by Jane.
4. The tree is being blown against the house by the wind.
5. The dog is usually fed by Jack.
6. Her appointment was canceled by the dentist.
7. The car should be repaired by the mechanic.
8. The clients have been called by the secretary.
9. The fireworks are going to be set off by him.
10. The game is going to be postponed by the coach.
11. That portrait was painted by Jack.
12. I am being helped by the salesperson.
13. The children will be taken care of by their grandmother.
14. The mess should be cleaned up by the person who made it.
15. A movie animation system called Contour was invented by Steve Perlman.

Discussion with your partner.
Answers vary. Examples of possible sentences:
Tomatoes are grown in my country. Celery is grown in my country.
Cows are raised in my country.
Good food is made in my country.
Cars are manufactured in my country.
Paper was invented in China.

Page 77
Answers vary. Examples of possible sentences for set #1:
1. If I win $1,000,000, I will donate money to charity.
2. I drive carefully.
3. He should go to the dentist.
4. No, I have not arrived late to a movie. OR: No, I have never arrived late to a movie. OR: Yes, I have arrived late to a movie. Yes, I have often arrived late to a movie.
5. Swim fins were invented in the United States by Benjamin Franklin.

Page 78
Answers vary. Example #1. Drive (or walk) along Hollywood Boulevard to Vine Street. Turn left. Walk up Vine Street and you'll see Capitol Records on the right.

Page 81-82
Answers vary. Example #1. Drive (or walk) up Normandie Avenue to Franklin Boulevard. The Fitness Center is on the corner.

Page 84
1. D
2. J
3. E
4. G
5. A
6. C
7. B
8. I
9. F
10. H

Page 87
1. B
2. A
3. E
4. C
5. D
6. J
7. I
8. F
9. G
10. H
11. M
12. O
13. L
14. K
15. N
16. R
17. S
18. P

19. T
20. Q

True or False
1. F
2. T
3. T
4. F
5. F

Page 94
Set #1
1. D
2. B
3. A
4. F
5. C
6. E
7. H
8. I
9. J
10. L
11. G
12. K
13. Q
14. R
15. N
16. M
17. O
18. P

Set #2
1. E
2. C
3. F
4. A
5. D
6. B
7. L
8. J
9. K
10. I
11. H
12. G
13. O
14. Q
15. N
16. R
17. P
18. M

Page 95 Reading Comprehension
1. Juan Rodriguez Cabrillo
2. 1542; Santa Catalina Island
3. They welcomed him.
4. The Gabrielinos.
5. The Tataviam.
6. The Chumash.
7. Shell beads.
8. The shell bead money makers.
9. Pine pitch, asphalt, and redwood.
10. Acorns.
11. Limitation, moderation, and compensation.
12. Two smallpox epidemics.
13. 1848.
14. 1850.
15. To bring attention to the First People (Native Americans).
16. *Ramona*. A love story about a rich Mexican girl and a Tataviam worker.
17. No, it did not.
18. They work in their casinos.

Page 99
Set #1
1. E
2. C
3. D
4. B
5. A
6. H
7. I
8. F
9. J
10. G

Set #2
1. B
2. E
3. A
4. C
5. D
6. H
7. J
8. F
9. G
10. I

Page 105
Set #1
1. E
2. C
3. A
4. D
5. B
6. G
7. I
8. J
9. F
10. H
11. N
12. M
13. K
14. O
15. L

Set #2
1. E
2. A
3. D
4. C
5. F
6. B
7. H
8. K
9. J
10. I
11. G
12. O
13. P
14. M
15. N
16. L

Page 105 Reading Comprehension
1. Avila Adobe; Olvera Street; 1818.
2. The Tongva (Native Americans).
3. Northwestern Mexico.
4. 44.
5. Two. Mixed ethnic groups: Native American, African, European.
6. The Italians, the French, and the Chinese.
7. The last Mexican governor (1845-1846).
8. 1850.
9. A businesswoman, landowner, and former slave who won her freedom in court. You can learn about her at the Biddy Mason Park.
10. Mexican Americans.

Page 106
1. E
2. B
3. F
4. C
5. A
6. D

Page 110
Set #1
1. D
2. C
3. B
4. F
5. A
6. E

Set #2
1. E
2. C
3. A
4. B
5. D
6. H
7. J
8. G
9. I
10. F
11. O
12. N
13. L
14. P
15. M

Page 114
Set #1
1. C
2. A
3. F
4. E
5. D
6. B
7. J
8. I
9. H
10. G
11. M
12. K
13. R
14. P
15. S
16. Q
17. O
18. N

Set #2
1. E
2. A
3. F
4. C
5. D
6. B
7. G
8. L
9. H
10. J
11. K
12. M

171

13. P
14. N
15. Q
16. R
17. O

Page 117
1. E
2. F
3. A
4. B
5. D
6. C

Page 118
Across
5. renovate
6. damage
8. extinct
11. resource
13. philosophy
14. slave
19. dishonor
21. prosperous
23. remain
24. principle
25. fiction
27. settlement
28. adoption

Down
1. commercially
2. scavenger
3. compensation
4. heritage
7. materialistic
9. discover
10. allow
12. approval
15. asphalt
16. greed
17. hire
18. illegal
19. destroy
20. recognize
22. suffer
25. found
26. claim

Page 122
1. D
2. F
3. E
4. B
5. A
6. C
7. L
8. K
9. I
10. J
11. H
12. G
13. S
14. N
15. M
16. O
17. Q
18. P
19. R

Page 125
1. E
2. D
3. A
4. C
5. B
6. G
7. H
8. I
9. F
10. J
11. L
12. O
13. M
14. K
15. N
16. S
17. T
18. P
19. Q
20. R
21. X
22. W
23. Z
24. V
25. Y
26. U

True or False
1. F
2. T
3. T
4. F
5. T

Page 127
Answers vary

Page 129
1. C
2. E
3. A
4. B
5. D
6. F
7. H
8. G
9. M
10. L
11. I
12. J
13. K

True or False
1. F
2. F
3. F
4. T
5. F

Page 134
1. B
2. E
3. A
4. C
5. D
6. G
7. F
8. K
9. H
10. I
11. J
12. P
13. Q
14. M
15. N
16. O
17. L

Page 136
Set #1
1. B
2. C
3. A

Set #2
1. H
2. K
3. D
4. E
5. G
6. A
7. J
8. F
9. B
10. C
11. I

Page 138
1. He admitted going to the beach.
2. She avoided going to the beach.
3. They appreciated going to the beach.
4. He asked to go to the beach.
5. I can go to the beach.
6. She always chooses to go to the beach.
7. You should consider going to the beach.
8. They couldn't go to the beach.
9. We decided to go to the beach.
10. She dislikes going to the beach.
11. We all enjoy going to the beach.
12. Don't expect to go to the beach.
13. She made her brother go to the beach.
14. They finished going to the beach.
15. I hope to go to the beach.
16. Imagine going to the beach.
17. I would like to keep going to the beach.
18. He always likes to go to the beach. OR: He always likes going to the beach.
19. They managed to go to the beach.
20. I might go to the beach.
21. You must go to the beach.
22. I don't need to go to the beach.
23. You should plan to go to the beach.
24. They promised to go to the beach.
25. Never quit going to the beach.
26. They recommend going to the beach.
27. She refuses to go to the beach.
28. Should I go to the beach?
29. He suggested going to the beach.
30. Do you want to go to the beach?
31. If it's sunny, they will go to the beach.
32. When she was a child, she would go to the beach.
33. He would like to go to the beach.
34. His mother let him go to the beach.

Page 140
1. B
2. F
3. C
4. A
5. D
6. E
7. J
8. I
9. G

10. L
11. H
12. K
13. Q
14. M
15. P
16. R
17. O
18. N

Page 142
1. D
2. E
3. F
4. C
5. B
6. A
7. K
8. I
9. G
10. H
11. L
12. J
13. O
14. P
15. N
16. M
17. R
18. Q

Page 145
1. K
2. L
3. F
4. E
5. N
6. A
7. B
8. I
9. M
10. D
11. C
12. H
13. G
14. J

Page 150
1. in
2. on
3. ---; on; on (or "at" if you are talking about the point where Wilshire Boulevard crosses at an intersection)
4. off; at
5. in
6. in (or "into")
7. ---
8. ---; in
9. at; at; on
10. in; in
11. to; on; at
12. on
13. On; at; in

14. during; In
15. at; in
16. in; at; in
17. on; in
18. at; on
19. in; --
20. in

Page 153
1. F
2. B
3. A
4. E
5. D
6. C
7. K
8. I
9. L
10. H
11. J
12. G
13. S
14. R
15. Q
16. N
17. P
18. O
19. M

Web exploration: Check the Internet for up-to-date answers.

Page 155
1. E
2. D
3. B
4. C
5. A
6. K
7. H
8. F
9. J
10. I
11. G

Page 156
Web exploration: Check the Internet for up-to-date answers.

Page 159
Reading comprehension:
1. "To inspire and nurture the human spirit—one person, one cup and one neighborhood at t time."
2. Jerry Baldwin, Zev Siegl, and Gordon Bowker in 1970.
3. Jerry Baldwin was an English teacher, Zev Siegl was a history teacher, and Gordon Bowker was a writer.
4. They named it after the character Starbucks in *Moby Dick* by Herman Melville.
5. Howard Schultz. He started selling coffee as they do in Italy.
6. They make sure that the coffee is grown in a sustainable way, and that all their workers are paid enough.
7. They are changing to LED light bulbs.
8. On the Internet.

Vocabulary
1. D
2. E
3. B
4. C
5. A
6. I
7. J
8. G
9. F
10. H
11. K

Page 161
Across
1. philosophy
2. intolerant
4. confide
6. public
7. duty
10. debt
12. find
13. mature
14. wild
17. immigrant
20. settle
21. poisoning
22. environment
24. guard
25. founder
27. release
28. migrant

Down
1. prohibit
3. mood
5. exhibit
8. trust
9. design
11. extinct
15. destroy
16. fascinating
18. available
19. endangered
21. possess
23. product
26. lecture

173

Picture Credits

CC=Creative Commons Attribution-Share Alike. Creativecommons.org
GNU=GNU Free Documentation License. En.wikipedia.org/wiki/GNU_Free_Documentation_License
PD=Public Domain
Images from Office.microsoft.com are the property of Microsoft. Thank you, Microsoft!

cover page	Fumagalli, Barbara. Cover design. 2012. Ink, pencil, and oil painting.
i +	*Elephant*. Clipart. n.d. Drawing. *Office.microsoft.com*. Web. 28 May 2011.
1	*1996 Chevrolet Camaro in Venice, California.jpg*. 2004. Photograph. Venice, California. *Commons.wikimedia.org*. Web. 02 Sept. 2012. (CC) Serouj (name of author). *Downtown LA from Griffith Park.jpg*. 18 Dec. 2006. Photograph. Los Angeles. Uploaded on 19 December 2006. *Commons.wikimedia.org*. Web. 9 Oct. 2011. (PD)
2	Stickpin (name of author). *Descansogardens1.jpg*. 17 June 2009. Photograph. La Cañada-Flintridge, CA. Uploaded on 18 June 2009. *Commons.wikimedia.org*. Web. 13 June 2011. (PD)
4	Chung, Yoo. *Expo Bridge (from North End).jpg*. 29 Apr. 2007. Photograph. Expo Science Park, Daejeon, South Korea. Uploaded 28 May 2007. *Commons.wikimedia.org*. Web. 14 June 2011. (CC) 北纬30度, *Harbin No.3 High School.JPG*. Photograph. 21 Dec. 2008. Uploaded 7 Dec. 2009. *Commons.wikimedia.org*. Web. 5 Feb. 2012. (PD) Manrique, Daniel. *Palacio Bellas Artes Desde Torre Latino.jpg*. 18 Sept. 2006. Photograph. Mexico City. Uploaded 18 Sept. 2006. *Commons.wikimedia.org*. Web. 11 Oct. 2011. (GNU – CC) Marcel, Baptiste. *P-AD20061109-13h03m11s-g.jpg*. 9 Nov. 2006. Photograph. Masmak Castle, Riyadh, Saudi Arabia. Uploaded 20 Nov. 2006. *Commons.wikimedia.org*. Web. 11 Nov. 2011. (PD)
5	Cors (Name of Author). *Tokyo Odaiba.jpg*. 13 Aug. 2007. Photograph. Tokyo Odaiba, Japan. *Commons.wikimedia.org*. Web. 11 Oct. 2011. (GNU – CC) Kallgan (name of author). *Beijing Hutong 2005-3.JPG*. 8 Oct. 2005. Photograph. *Commons.wikimedia.org*. Web. 12 Oct. 2011. (PD)
6	Plotz, Joseph. *Hancock Park Street.JPG*. 22 May 2010. Photograph. A Street in Hancock Park, Los Angeles. Uploaded on 18 June 2010. *Commons.wikimedia.org*. Web. 11 Oct. 2011. (GNU – CC)
7	*Cell Phone*. Clipart. n.d. Photograph. *Office.microsoft.com*. Web. 21 June 2011. *Cruise Ship*. Clipart. n.d. Photograph. *Office.microsoft.com*. Web. 21 June 2011. Deleon, Danielle. *Degaen.jpg* (Chihuahua). 28 Oct. 2008. Photograph. Uploaded on 2 Nov. 2008. *Commons.wikimedia.org*. Web. 11 Oct. 2011. (CC) *German Shepherd*. Clipart. n.d. Photograph. *Office.microsoft.com*. Web. 21 June 2011. *Picnic Basket*. Clipart. n.d. Photograph. *Office.microsoft.com*. Web. 21 June 2011. *Set Table in Resaurant*. Clipart. n.d. Photograph. *Office.microsoft.com*. Web. 21 June 2011. *Telephone, Land Line*. Clipart. n.d. Photograph. *Office.microsoft.com*. Web. 21 June 2011. *Train, Oberstorf, Bavaria*. Clipart. n.d. Photograph. *Office.microsoft.com*. Web. 21 June 2011.
8	*Black Widow Spider*. Clipart. n.d. Drawing. *Office.microsoft.com*. Web. 29 May 2011. *Snake*. Clipart. n.d. Drawing. *Office.microsoft.com*. Web. 29 May 2011.
10	*Businessmen*. Clipart. n.d. Drawing. *Office.microsoft.com*. Web. 25 May 2011. *Engineer*. Clipart. n.d. Drawing. *Office.microsoft.com*. Web. 25 May 2011. *Mechanic*. Clipart. n.d. Drawing. *Office.microsoft.com*. Web. 28 May 2011. Sullivan, Jon. *Orleans.Bourbon.Arp.750pix.jpg*. 4 Sept. 2005. Photograph. Bourbon Street, New Orleans, Louisiana. *Commons.wikimedia.org*. Web. 5 Feb. 2012. (PD) Trischler, M. *Manhattan3 amk.jpg*. Sept. 2007. Photograph. Uploaded on 27 March 2008. *Commons.wikimedia.org*. Web. 11 Oct. 2011. (CC)
14	*Girl Fishing, Painter, Roses*. Clipart. n.d. Photographs. *Office.microsoft.com*. Web. 22 Dec. 2012. Gomes, Edgar. *Pyramidgise.jpg*.29 Aug. 2010. Photograph. Giza Pyramid Complex, Egypt. *Commons.wikimedia.org*. Web. 23 Dec. 2012. (PD)
15	*Flowers*. Clipart. n.d. Drawings. *Office.microsoft.com*. Web. 27 May 2011.
18	Kay, Kelvin. *Melrose4.jpg: Partial Melrose Avenue, Los Angeles, CA*. 10 Apr. 2004. Photograph. Los Angeles. *Commons.wikimedia.org*. Web. 24 Dec. 2012. (GNU)
19	*Cherries*. Clipart. n.d. Photograph. *Office.microsoft.com*. Web. 27 May 2011. Fritz (author). *Raw Cane Sugar Light.jpg*. 22 Feb. 2009. Photograph. *Commons.wikimedia.org*. Web. 25 Dec. 2012. (GNU-CC)
20	*Notepad*. Clipart. n.d. Drawing. *Office.microsoft.com*. Web. 28 May 2011.
24	Ikezaki, Fabio. *Michael Jackson's Star*. 23 Feb 2008. Photograph. *Flickr.com*. Web. 27 May 2011. (CC) White House Photo Office. *Michael Jackson 1984(2).jpg*. 14 May 1984. Photograph. *Commons.wikimedia.org*. Web. 16 Jan. 2012. (PD)
25	L., Andy. *Janet Jackson 4.jpg*. 10 Sep. 2008. Photograph. *Commons.wikimedia.org*. Web. 16 Jan. 2012. Background removed by Pierre Zubrinsky. (CC)
28	*Plants, Animals, Solar Panel*. Clipart. n.d. Drawings. *Office.microsoft.com*. Web. 27 May 2011. Sanbeck, Ellen. *Lizard179*. 1992. Drawing. *Animal Silhouettes: 310 Royalty-Free Designs*. Mineola: Dover Publications, 2003. Print.

34	Belski, Carol, NPS. *Hiking Group.jpg*. 31 May 2005. Photograph. *Commons.wikimedia.org*. Web. 13 Oct. 2011. (PD) Hiser, David. *Using Mountain Climbing Techniques While Hiking in the Maze a Remote and Rugged Region in the Heart of the... - NARA - 545777.jpg*. May 1972. Photograph. Canyonlands National Park, Utah. *Commons.wikimedia.org*. Web. 13 Oct. 2011. (PD) Qoo Monster (author). *Flying a Kite near Golden Gate Bridge.jpg*. 21 Mar. 2005. Photograph. *Commons.wikimedia.org*. Web. 13 Oct. 2011. (CC) Schnell, Bryan, Sgt. 1st Class. *US Navy 080801-A-1528S-030 he Command Master Chief of Pre-Commissioning Unit George H.W. Bush (CVN 77), Jon D. Port, dives tandem with the Army's Golden Knights parachute team.jpg*. 1 Aug. 2008. Photograph. College Station, Texas. Uploaded on 22 Oct. 2009. *Commons.wikimedia.org*. Web. 13 Oct. 2011. (PD)
35	Ljsurf (author). *Makingthedrop.jpg*. 24 Dec. 2006. Photograph. California. *Commons.wikimedia.org*. Web. 12 Feb. 2012. (PD)
39	Studio Publicity Still (author), *Taylor,_Elizabeth_posed.jpg*. 1955 (?). Photograph. California. *Commons.wikimedia.org*. Web. 29 Jan. 2012. (PD)
40	*Mother and Daughter Preparing Food in a Mixing Bowl*. Clipart. n.d. Photograph. *Office.microsoft.com*. Web. 5 Aug. 2011. *Two Timepieces, One Set at 9 o'Clock and One Set at 5 o'Clock*. Clipart. n.d. Photograph. *Office.microsoft.com*. Web. 5 Aug. 2011. *Phone*. Clipart. n.d. Photograph. *Office.microsoft.com*. Web. 5 Aug. 2011.
41	*Two Timepieces, One Set at 9 o'Clock and One Set at 5 o'Clock*. Clipart. n.d. Photograph. *Office.microsoft.com*. Web. 5 Aug. 2011.
42	*Airports*. Clipart. n.d. Photograph. *Office.microsoft.com*. Web. 21 June 2011. *Businessmen*. Clipart. n.d. Photograph. *Office.microsoft.com*. Web. 21 June 2011. *Business Women*. Clipart. n.d. Photograph. *Office.microsoft.com*. Web. 21 June 2011. *Couples*. Clipart. n.d. Photograph. *Office.microsoft.com*. Web. 21 June 2011. *Girl Eating a Hotdog with Mustard and Ketchup*. Clipart. n.d. Photograph. *Office.microsoft.com*. Web. 21 June 2011. *Male Food Service Person at Work Holding a Takeout Bag and Soda*. Clipart. n.d. Photograph. *Office.microsoft.com*. Web. 21 June 2011.
44	*Eagle*. Clipart. n.d. Drawing. *Office.microsoft.com*. Web. 30 May. 2011. *Profiles*. Clipart. n.d. Drawing. *Office.microsoft.com*. Web. 30 May. 2011.
49	*Close-up of a Yellow and White Birthday Cake*. Clipart. n.d. Photograph. *Office.microsoft.com*. Web. 13 Oct. 2011. *Woman Showing Frustration While on the Telephone*. Clipart. n.d. Photograph. *Office.microsoft.com*. Web. 28 May 2011.
51	*Woman* (Advice Columnist). Clipart. n.d. Photograph. *Office.microsoft.com*. Web. 29 May 2011.
56	*Spades, Clubs, Hearts, Diamonds,and Note*. Clipart. n.d. Drawings. *Office.microsoft.com*. Web. 8 Jan. 2012.
58	Fink, K. *Mountain-Lion-01623.jpg*. 8 May 2008. Photograph. Yellowstone National Park. *Commons.wikimedia.org*. Web. 13. Oct. 2011. (PD)
59	Fumagalli, Barbara. *Solving a Problem in the Santa Monica Mountains*. 13 Oct. 2011. Drawing. Print. Printed with permission from the artist.
62	*Police*. Clipart. n.d. Photograph. *Office.microsoft.com*. Web. 28 May 2011.
69	*Men and Women*. Clipart. n.d. Photographs. *Office.microsoft.com*. Web. 21 June 2011.
71	*Deserted Island with Palm Trees*. Clipart. n.d. Photograph. *Office.microsoft.com*. Web. 18 Dec. 2012.
72	FEMA News Photo. *FEMA - 1676 - Photograph by FEMA News Photo taken on 01-17-1994 in California.jpg*. 17 Jan. 1994. Photograph. Northridge, California. Uploaded 14 Oct. 2009. *Commons.wikimedia.org*. Web. 13 Oct. 2011. (PD) John C. Stennis Space Center, National Aeronautics and Space Administration (NASA). *Loxosceles Reclusa.jpg*. Date unknown. Photograph. Uploaded on 15 May 2005. *Commons.wikimedia.org*. Web. 13 Oct. 2011. (PD) Reusch, Pascal. *Glass Floor of the CN Tower.JPG*. 7 Aug. 2004. Photograph. CN Tower, Toronto, Canada. Commons.wikimedia.org. Web. 13 Oct. 2011. (GNU – CC)
74	*Boy Playing Baseball*. Clipart. n.d. Photograph. *Office.microsoft.com*. Web. 29 May 2011.
78	*Person Icon with Arrows Out*. Clipart. n.d. Image. *Office.microsoft.com*. Web. 8 Jan. 2013.
79	Adrian 104 (author). *Hollywood Sign*. 7 July 2006. Photograph. Hollywood, California. Commons.wikimedia.org. Web. 2 Jan. 2013. (PD) Dunn, Andrew. *Capitol Records Building LA.jpg*. 6 May 2005. Photograph. Hollywood, California. Commons.wikimedia.org. Web. 2 Jan. 2013. (CC) Highsmith, Carol M. *Grauman's Chinese Theatre, by Carol Highsmith.jpg*. 5 July 2004. Photograph. Hollywood, California. Commons.wikimedia.org. Web. 2 Jan. 2013. (PD) Los Angeles (author). *Crossroads of the World, Hollywood.JPG*. 31 May 2008. Photograph. Hollywood, California. Commons.wikimedia.org. Web. 2 Jan. 2013. (GNU – CC) Minnaert, Gary. *Musso&Franks 05.jpg*. 28 Dec. 2006. Photograph. Hollywood, California. Commons.wikimedia.org. Web. 2 Jan. 2013. (PD) ---. *RooseveltHotel03.jpg*. 16 Feb. 2007. Photograph. Hollywood, California. Commons.wikimedia.org. Web. 8 Jan. 2013. (PD) Praefcke, Andreas. *Hollywood Cinerama Dome.jpg*. Oct. 2008. Photograph. Hollywood, California. Commons.wikimedia.org. Web. 2 Jan. 2013. (GNU – CC) Taveneaux, Antoine. *Paramount Pictures Studio 4.jpg*. 13 Mar. 2011. Photograph. Los Angeles, California. Commons.wikimedia.org. Web. 2 Jan. 2013. (CC)
80	*Shops, Places, and Objects*. Clipart. n.d. Photographs. *Office.microsoft.com*. Web. 8 Jan. 2013.
81-2	*Person Icon with Arrows Out*. Clipart. n.d. Image. *Office.microsoft.com*. Web. 8 Jan. 2013.
83	Alarhu (author). *City Walk, Universal City.jpg*. 22 Nov. 2010. Photograph. Universal City, California. Commons.wikimedia.org. Web. 8 Jan. 2013. (PD)

84	ДиБгд. Megatherum DB.jpg. Drawing. Uploaded 22 July 2007. *Commons.wikimedia.org*. Web. 7 Aug. 2011. (PD) Bogdanov, Dmitry. Mammuthus trogontherii122DB.jpg. Drawing. 20 Apr. 2009. *Commons.wikimedia.org*. Web. 7 Aug. 2011. (GNU – CC) Foresman, Pearson Scott. *Bobcat (PSF).jpg*. Drawing. 12 Aug. 2007. *Commons.wikimedia.org*. Web. 7 Aug. 2011. (PD) ---. *Bison (PSF).jpg*. Drawing. 14 Aug. 2007. *Commons.wikimedia.org*. Web. 7 Aug. 2011. (PD) ---. *Coyote (PSF).png*. Drawing. 16 Dec. 2008. *Commons.wikimedia.org*. Web. 7 Aug. 2011. (PD) ---.. *Dromedary 2 (PSF).png*. Drawing. 20 Apr. 2009. *Commons.wikimedia.org*. Web. 7 Aug. 2011. (PD) ---.. *Horse (PSF).png*. Drawing. (Altered.) 22 Dec. 2007. *Commons.wikimedia.org*. Web. 7 Aug. 2011. (PD) ---.. *Sloth bear (PSF).png*. Drawing. 7 Dec. 2007. *Commons.wikimedia.org*. Web. 7 Aug. 2011. (PD) ---.. *Snow Leopard (PSF).png*. Drawing. (Altered.) 12 June. 2009. *Commons.wikimedia.org*. Web. 7 Aug. 2011. (PD) ---.. *Tiger 2 (PSF).png*. Drawing. (Altered.) 16 June. 2009. *Commons.wikimedia.org*. Web. 7 Aug. 2011. (PD) ---.. *Wolf (PSF).png*. Drawing. 16 June 2009. *Commons.wikimedia.org*. Web. 7 Aug. 2011. (PD) W. (initialed only). *Britannica Eagle-Sea Eagle.png*. Drawing. *Encyclopaedia Britannica*, 1911. Uploaded 4 Jan. 2011. *Commons.wikimedia.org*. Web. 7 Aug. 2011. (PD)
85	MyName (3scandal0) (author). *LaBreaTarPits01.JPG*. Photograph. 17 Nov. 2007. *Commons.wikimedia.org*. Web. 7 Jan. 2013. (PD)
86	Desoeuvre, Voyou. *Teratornis fossil.jpg*. Photograph. Page Museum. 10 July 2006. *Commons.wikimedia.org*. Web. 7 Aug. 2011. (CC) Reverendlukewarm (name of author). Teratornis merriami fossil.jpg. Photograph. La Brea Tar Pits. December 20, 2009. Uploaded Sept. 20, 2010. Commons.wikimedia.org. Web. Sept. 21, 2011. (CC) Wallace63 (name of author). *Smilodon head.jpg*. Photograph. American Natural History Museum, NY. Uploaded 28 Oct. 2008. *Commons.wikimedia.org*. Web. 7 Aug. 2011. (GNU – CC)
90	Fumagalli, Piera. *Map of the First People in Los Angeles*. 2011. Drawing. Print. *Tongva woman.jpg*, Tongva (Gabrielino) *Mrs. James V. Rosemeyre; Bakersfield*. July 1905. Photograph. From the C. Hart Merriam Collection of Native American Photographs, Bancroft Library, UC Berkeley. *Commons.wikimedia.org*. Web. 17 Oct. 2012. (PD-US)
91	Fumagalli, Piera. *An Ap, or Chumash House, at the Chumash Museum in Thousand Oaks*. 2010. Photograph. JPG file. Jengod (author). *Tongvaki.jpg*. 11 Apr. 2012. Photograph. (Replica at Franklin Canyon Park in the Santa Monica Mountains.) *Commons.wikimedia.org*. Web. 8 Jan. 2013. (GNU – CC) Schwemmer, Robert, CINMS, NOS, NOAA. *Sanc0157 - Flickr - NOAA Photo Library.jpg*. 2006, Uploaded 9 Jan. 2012. Photograph. (Chumash Tomol 'Elye'wun, Santa Cruz Island. California.) From the NOAA Photo Library. *Commons.wikimedia.org*. Web. 17 Oct. 2012. (PD)
92	Daderot (author). *Basketry tray, Chumash, Santa Barbara Mission, early 1800s - Native American collection - Peabody Museum, Harvard University - DSC05558.JPG*. Photograph (Uploaded by Daderot). USA. 18 Mar. 2012. From the Native American Collection, Peabody Museum, Harvard University, Cambridge, Massachusetts. *Commons.wikimedia.org*. Web. 17 Oct. 2012. (PD – CC)
93	NeoPrometheusX (Author). *DSC04912.JPG*. Photograph. (Reconstructed Chumash house at the Satwiwa Natural Area a.k.a Rancho Guadalasca). 23 Feb. 2012. Web. 17 Oct. 2012. (GNU – CC)
94	*Acorn, Shell, and Beads*. Clipart. n.d. Drawings. *Office.microsoft.com*. Web. 27 May 2011.
96	*Necessary and Unnecessary Objects*. Clipart. n.d. Photographs. *Office.microsoft.com*. Web. 27 May 2011.
97	*States and Umbrella*. Clipart. n.d. Drawings. *Office.microsoft.com*. Web. 27 May 2011.
98	*Map of the United States*. Clipart. n.d. Drawing. *Office.microsoft.com*. Web. 27 May 2011.
100	*1920 Alta California Mission Trail.jpg: An Early Map Illustrating the Route of "El Camino Real" and the 21 Franciscan Missions in 1821*. 30 Oct. 2006. Drawing. Scanned from: *California from the Conquistadores to the Legends of Laguna. Commons.wikimedia.org*. Web. 9 June 2011. (GNU – CC)
101	Denney, Ewen. *El Camino Real California 2.jpg*. 16 Jan. 2005. Photograph. Santa Clara, California. *Commons.wikimedia.org*. Web. 9 June 2011. (GNU – CC)
102	Los Angeles (name of author). *Avila Adobe, Olvera Street, Los Angeles.JPG*. May 2008. Photograph. Olvera Street, Los Angeles, California. *Commons.wikimedia.org*. Web. 10 Jan. 2013. (GNU – CC)
103	Gagnon, Brenard. *Avila Adobe02.jpg, Avila Adobe Kitchen*. 7 Sept. 2008. Photograph . Olvera Street, Los Angeles, California. *Commons.wikimedia.org*. Web. 10 Jan. 2013. (GNU – CC)
104	Fumagalli, Piera. *La Placita Church (Nuestra Señora Reina de los Angeles Asistencia)*. 7 Jan. 2012. Photograph. Main Street, Los Angeles. JPG file. Fumagalli, Piera. *A Mosaic Reproduction of a Detail of the Painting in Assisi*. 7 Jan. 2012. Photograph. From the façade of La PlacitaChurch, Main Street, Los Angeles. JPG file. Fumagalli, Piera. *Pico House*. 7 Jan. 2012. Photograph. Olvera Street, Los Angeles. JPG file. Schumacher, Los Angeles. *Pío Pico cph.31737.jpg, Pio Pico, Governor of Mexican Los Angeles*. 1897. Photograph. Uploaded 31 July 2011 *Commons.wikimedia.org*. Web. 10 Jan. 2013. (PD)
105	*Bricks*. Clipart. n.d. Drawings. *Office.microsoft.com*. Web. 10 Feb. 2013. *Vine*. Clipart. n.d. Drawings. *Office.microsoft.com*. Web. 10 Feb. 2013.
106	Fumagalli, Piera. *Olvera Street Sign*. 7 Jan. 2012. Photograph. Olvera Steet, Los Angeles. JPG file.
107	Fumagalli, Piera. *Olvera Street*. 7 Jan. 2012. Photograph. Olvera Steet, Los Angeles. JPG file.
108	Detroit Publishing Company. *Mission San Fernando Postcard, circa 1900.jpg*. 1900-Photograph. Uploaded 8 Apr. 2008. *Commons.wikimedia.org*. Web. 9 June 2011. (PD) Geographer (author). *2007 Mission San Fernando.jpg*. 30 March 2007. Photo. *Commons.wikimedia.org*. 9 June 2011. (CC) ---. *Exterior of Mission San Fernando Rey de España MSF 033.jpg*. 30 March 2007. Photograph. *Commons.wikimedia.org*. 9 June 2011. (CC)

109	Geographer (name of author). *Corridor at Mission San Fernando Rey de Espana.jpg.* 30 March 2007. Photograph. *Commons.wikimedia.org.* 9 June 2011. (CC)
110	*Animals and Plants.* Clipart. n.d. Drawings. *Office.microsoft.com.* Web. 27 May 2011.
111	Los Angeles (name of author). *Leonis Adobe, Calabasas (2008).JPG.* 29 Apr. 2008. Photograph. *Commons.wikimedia.org.* Web. 10 June 2011. (GNU – CC)
113	*Snake (Altered), Pumpkins and Squash.* Clipart. n.d. Drawings. *Office.microsoft.com.* Web. 27 May 2011.
114	*Goat.* Clipart. n.d. Drawing. *Office.microsoft.com.* Web. 27 May 2011.
115	Los Angeles (name of author). *Courtyard at Romulo Pico Adobe, Mission Hills.JPG.* 29 Apr. 2008. Photograph. *Commons.wikimedia.org.* Web. 11 June 2001. (GNU – CC)
116	Los Angeles (name of author). *Orcutt Ranch gate.jpg.* 28 Sept. 2008. Photograph. *Commons.wikimedia.org.* Web. 11 June 2011. (CC-GNU)
117	*Oak Tree.* Clipart. n.d. Drawing. *Office.microsoft.com.* Web. 27 May 2011. Sanbeck, Ellen. *Coyote020.* 1992. Drawing. *Animal Silhouettes: 310 Royalty-Free Designs.* Mineola: Dover Publications, 2003. Print.
120	*Captain_Jack.jpg.* 1864 (uploaded by Gentgeen 1 Dec. 2003). Photograph. Modoc Chief Kintpuash, northeastern California. *Commons.wikimedia.org.* Web. 8 Jan. 2013. (PD) Daderot (author). *800px-Whistle,_Chumash,_from_Bowers'_Cave,_collected_1885_-_Native_American_collection_-_Peabody_Museum,_Harvard_University_-_DSC05556.jpg.* 18 Mar. 2012. Photograph. *Commons.wikimedia.org.* Web. 8 Jan. 2013. (CC – PD) *Home on the Prairie.jpg.* (Movie poster of Home on the Prairie, 1939, starring Gene Autry). 1939. Source: WWW.cinemasterpieces.com. Uploaded 23 May 2011. *Commons.wikimedia.org.* Web. 11 June 2011. (PD) Minnaert, Gary. *AutryCenter 01.jpg.* 28 Dec. 2006. Photograph. Autry National Center, Museum of the American West in Griffith Park, Los Angeles, CA. *Commons.wikimedia.org.* Web. 11 June 2011. (PD) National Parks Service (author). *Basket_of_Basketmaker_Pueblo_people.jpg* 9 Oct. 2006. Photograph. *Commons.wikimedia.org.* Web. 8 Jan. 2013. (PD)
121	Kane, Joseph. *Champion in Oh, Susanna!.png.* 1936. Photograph from the movie *Oh, Susanna!* Uploaded 23 July 2009. *Commons.wikimedia.org.* Web. 11 June 2011. (PD) ---. *Gene Autry in Oh, Susanna!.png.* 1936. Photograph from the movie *Oh, Susanna!* Uploaded 23 July 2009. *Commons.wikimedia.org.* Web. 11 June 2011. (PD)
122	*Horse's Hoof from a Horse.* Clipart. n.d. Drawing. *Office.microsoft.com.* Web. 27 May 2011.
123	Xurble (name of author). *Los Angeles Zoo.jpg (Los Angeles Zoo Entry).* 5 Apr. 2007. Photograph. *Commons.wikimedia.org.* Web. 12 June 2011. (CC)
124	*Meerkats.* Clipart. n.d. Photograph. *Office.microsoft.com.* Web. 13 June 2011. Quinn, Michael (aka Grand Canyon NPS). *Grand Canyon CA Condor #87 _3467.* 18 May 2011. Photograph. Grand Canyon. *Flickr.com.* Web. 4 June 2011. (CC) ---. *Grand Canyon CA Condor #87 _3462.* 18 May 2011. Photograph. Grand Canyon. *Flickr.com.* Web. 4 June 2011. (CC) ---. *Grand Canyon CA Condor #87 _3515.* 18 May 2011. Photograph. Grand Canyon. *Flickr.com.* Web. 4 June 2011. (CC)
126	*Plants and Animals.* Clipart. n.d. Drawings. *Office.microsoft.com.* Web. 13 June 2011. Sanbeck, Ellen. *Cougar173.* 1992. Drawing. *Animal Silhouettes: 310 Royalty-Free Designs.* Mineola: Dover Publications, 2003. Print. ---. *Wolf178.* 1992. Drawing. *Animal Silhouettes: 310 Royalty-Free Designs.* Mineola: Dover Publications, 2003. Print.
127	*Plants.* Clipart. n.d. Drawings. *Office.microsoft.com.* Web. 13 June 2011.
128	Field, Matthew. *Griffith Observatory.jpg.* 15 Sept. 2006. Photograph. Los Angeles. Uploaded on 27 Mar. 2007. *Commons.wikimedia.org.* Web. 13. June 2011. (GNU – CC)
129	*Hawk.* Clipart. n.d. Drawing. *Office.microsoft.com.* Web. 13 June 2011.
130	Forrestn (name of author). *Getty Center Grounds 018.jpg.* 10 Jan. 2008. Photograph. *Wikimediacommons.org.* Web. 27 Mar. 2013. (PD)
131	da Conegliano, Cima. *A Saint on Horseback, Paul Getty Museum.jpg.* 1460-1518. Uploaded 6 July 2010. Red chalk drawing. The J. Paul Getty Museum, Los Angeles. *Wikimediacommons.org.* Web. 17 Feb. 2013. (PD) van Gogh, Vincent.*Irises - Gogh, Vincent van - Irises - Google Art Project.jpg.* 1889. Uploaded 18 Oct. 2012. Oil on canvas. The J. Paul Getty Museum, Los Angeles. *Wikimediacommons.org.* Web. 17 Feb. 2013. (PD)
132	Mathis, Remi (photographer). Leogros Group (artists). *Getty Villa - Storage Jar with Aeneas and Anchises - inv. 86.AE.82.jpg.* 510 BCE. Uploaded 13 Dec. 2011. Photograph of Greek terracotta. The Getty Villa, Pacific Palisades, CA. *Wikimediacommons.org.* Web. 17 Feb. 2013. (CC)
133	Ha'Eri, Bobak. *060807-002-GettyVilla001.jpg.* 8 June 2007. Photograph. Malibu, CA. Uploaded 11 June 2007. *Commons.wikimedia.org.* Web. 15 June 2011. (CC) Hill, Dave, and Margie Kleerup.*Bust of a Youth (repro of Roman bronze from 1C AD at Villa dei Papiri, Herculaneum - Getty Villa - Outer Peristyle.jpg.* 27 Dec. 2010. Bronze sculpture. The Getty Villa, Pacific Palisades, CA. *Wikimediacommons.org.* Web. 17 Feb. 2013. (CC)
135	Fumagalli, Piera. *Leo Carrillo Beach.* 2010. Photograph. Leo Carrillo Beach, Malibu. JPG file.
136	*Anemone, Shell, and Starfish.* Clipart. n.d. Drawings. *Office.microsoft.com.* Web. 13 June 2011. Jelson25 (name of author). *Venice Beach Street Performer.jpg.* 21 July 2009. Photograph. Venice, CA. Uploaded on 29 July 2009. *Commons.wikimedia.org.* Web. 14 June 2011. (PD)
138	Fumagalli, Piera. *Tidepool on Leo Carrillo Beach.* 2010. Photograph. Leo Carrillo Beach, Malibu. JPG file.
139	*Denimjeans2.JPG.* 15 Oct. 2008. Photograph. Uploaded on 4 Nov. 2009. *Commons.wikimedia.org.* Web. 15 June 2011. (GNU – CC)

141	Bjankuloski06 (name of author). *Phantom IV.jpg*. 16 Feb. 2007. Photograph. Uploaded on 1 Sept. 2009. *Commons.wikimedia.org*. Web. 15 June 2011. (PD) *1955 Mercedes-Benz 300SL Gullwing Coupe 34.jpg - from the Ralph Lauren Collection*. 25 Apr. 2005. Photograph. Boston Museum of Fine Arts, Boston.*Commons.wikimedia.org*. Web. 15 June 2011. (GNU – CC)
142	*Gull*. Clipart (altered). n.d. Drawing. *Office.microsoft.com*. Web. 13 Jan. 2013.
143	Anderson, Erik. *450px-Farmers.jpg*. 2004. Photograph. Later uploaded by Geltoob 21 Aug. 2005 – 15 June 2009. *Commons.wikimedia.org*. Web. 28 June 2011. (PD)
144	Govan, Donovan. *Kitchen Funnel.jpg*. . 24 Apr. 2005. Photograph. Uploaded 26 Apr. 2005; rotated 23 Aug. 2009. *Commons.wikimedia.org*. Web. 28 June 2011. (GNU – CC) Ha'Eri, Bobak. *800px-052707-026-TheGrove.jpg*. Photograph. 27 May 2007. *Commons.wikimedia.org*. Web. 10 Jan. 2013. (CC) Lorax (name of author). *Funnel Cake 20040821 172200 1.1655x1275.jpg*. 23 Aug. 2004. Photograph. Later version uploaded by Pd THOR 24 Feb. 2009. *Commons.wikimedia.org*. Web. 28 June 2011. (GNU – CC)
145	*Fruits and Vegetables*. Clipart. n.d. Drawings. *Office.microsoft.com*. Web. 13 June 2011.
146	*Delores Del Rio*. (Photo by Piera Fumagalli.) 2011. Hollywood, CA. JPG file.. The mural *Dolores Del Rio* (on Hudson Avenue at 6529 Hollywood Boulevard) was painted in 1990 by Alfredo de Batuc with his assistants Arutyun Arutyunian, Johanna Coleman, Arlen Gutierrez, and James Stubbs. *Quinceanera* (Photo by Piera Fumagalli). 2011. Los Angeles, CA. JPG file. The mural *Quinceanera* (on Lemoyne Street at Sunset Boulevard) was painted in 1996 by Theresa Powers and her assistant Carolina Flores.
147	Garcia, Emmalee. *Union7 DSC 0200 EGarcia 2011.jpg*. 13 Oct. 2011. Photograph. *Commons.wikimedia.org*. Web. 19 Jan. 2013 (CC) Mackerm (name of author). *Union-Station-LA-Waiting-Ro.jpg*. 12 June 2004. Photograph. *Commons.wikimedia.org*. Web. 19 Jan. 2013. (GNU – CC) *Sculpting Another Destiny*. (Photo by Piera Fumagalli). 2011. Los Angeles, CA. JPG file. The mural *Sculpting Another Destiny* (on Sunset Boulevard at Echo Park Avenue) was painted in 2002 by Ricardo Mendoza and his assistants.
148	A Syn from California (author's name). *Revok MSK AWR SeventhLetter VA LosAngeles Graffiti Art.jpg*. 21 Apr. 2008. Photograph. Uploaded 3 Apr. 2010. *Commons.wikimedia.org*. Web. 4 Mar. 2013 (CC) Buchanan-Hermit (name of author). *Chinatown-la-overview2.jpg*. 18 May 2007. Photograph. *Commons.wikimedia.org*. Web. 19 Jan. 2013. © "The copyright holder of this file allows anyone to use it **for any purpose, provided that** the copyright holder is properly attributed. Redistribution, derivative work, commercial use, and all other use is permitted." Geographer (name of author) *Westin Bonaventure Hotel.jpg*. 31 Dec. 2006. Uploaded 17 July 2010. Photograph. As seen from the platform of 444 S. Flower Street, Los Angeles. *Wikimediacommons.org*. Web. 17 Feb. 2013. (GNU) Highsmith, Carol M. *Grauman's Chinese Theatre, by Carol Highsmith.jpg*. 5 July 2004. Photograph. Hollywood, California. Commons.wikimedia.org. Web. 2 Jan. 2013. (PD) Praefcke, Andreas. *LA Cathedral exterior 2.jpg*. Oct. 2008. Photograph. *Commons.wikimedia.org*. Web. 19 Jan. 2013. (GNU – CC) Sullivan, Jon. *800px-WaltDisneyConcertHall.jpg*. 21 May 2004. Photograph. *Commons.wikimedia.org*. Web. 19 Jan. 2013. (PD) Toksave (name of author). *Koyasan_Buddhist_Temple_Little_Tokyo_Los_Angeles.jpg*. 2006. Photograph. *Commons.wikimedia.org*. Web. 19 Jan. 2013. (GNU – CC)
151	Ebru (name of author). *800px-Fast_food_01_ebru.jpg*. 24 Feb. 2005. Photograph. *Commons.wikimedia.org*. Web. 10 Jan. 2013. (CC)
152	Brand, Gila. *BikurimS.jpg*. 25 June 2007. Photograph. *Commons.wikimedia.org*. Web. 10 Jan. 2013. (CC) Fangz (name of author). *North_Pacific_Gyre_World_Map.png*. 28 Oct. 2008. Map. *Commons.wikimedia.org*. Web. 10 Jan. 2013. (PD)
154	Hathorn, Billy. *800px-Chili's_in_Eagle_Pass_IMG_0268.jpg*. 27 July 2008. Photograph. *Commons.wikimedia.org*. Web. 10 Jan. 2013. (GNU – CC) Mchavez (name of author). *Fajitas-small.png*. 1 July 2009. Photograph. *Commons.wikimedia.org*. Web. 10 Jan. 2013. (CC)
155	*Chili Peppers*. Clipart. n.d. Photograph. *Office.microsoft.com*. Web. 22 June 2011.
157	Lopez, Johnny. *Cappuccino_with_foam.jpg*. 14 Oct. 2006. Photograph. *Commons.wikimedia.org*. Web. 25 Mar. 2013. (CC)
158	*Cinnamon*. Clipart. n.d. *Office.microsoft.com*. Web. 21 Oct. 2012. *E27 with 38 LCD.JPG*. (LED Light Bulb). 4 March 2006. Photograph. *Commons.wikimedia.org*. Web. 23 June 2011. *Giligone (name of author). Compact Fluorescent-bw.jpg. 17 September 2008. Photograph. Uploaded 12 March 2009. Commons.wikimedia.org. Web. 23 June 2011.* KMJ (name of author). Gluehlampe 01 KMJ.jpg (Incandescent Light Bulb). 26 June 2004. Photograph. Turkey. Uploaded 22 May 2011. Commons.wikimedia.org. Web. 23 June 2011. *Muskatnuss 02.jpg*. 20 May 2007. Photograph. Fotodatenbank.com Netherlands. *Commons.wikimedia.org*. Web. 23 June 2011. (PD) Nova (author/user). *Hazelnuts 02.jpg*. 2 Oct. 2005. Photograph. *Commons.wikimedia.org*. Web. 21 Oct. 2012. (GNU) *Strawberry*. Clipart. n.d. *Office.microsoft.com*. Web. 21 Oct. 2012. *Tuxedo*. Clipart. n.d. *Office.microsoft.com*. Web. 21 Oct. 2012. *Zebra*. Clipart. n.d. *Office.microsoft.com*. Web. 21 Oct. 2012.
160	Zenz, Rainer, *Laktoseintoleranz-1_svg #2.png*. 31 Aug. 2008. Map. Uploaded 22 July 2010. *Commons.wikimedia.org*. Web. 3 Mar. 2013. (PD)

Bibliography

"About Starbucks: History and Mission Statement." *Starbucks.com*. Starbucks Coffee Company, 2008. Web. 22 June 2011.

"Andres Pico Adobe." *Laparks.org*. City of Los Angeles Department of Recreation and Parks, 2011. Web. 11 June 2011.

"Andres Pico Adobe." Reprinted from *The Branding Iron* Dec. 1976. *Sfvhs.com*. The San Fernando Valley Historical Society, n.d. Web. 11 June 2011.

Armenta, Vincent. "*Amuyich* A Tradition of Giving." *Santainezchumash.org*. Santa Inez Band of Chumash Indians, 2009. Web. 10 Oct. 2012.

Autry. Theautry.org. Autry National Center, 2011. Web. 11 June 2011.

"Being a Responsible Company." *Starbucks.com*. Starbucks Corporation, n.d. (© 2012). Web. 10 Oct. 2012.

Berry, Beth. "Can I Reuse a Plastic Water Bottle Over & Over?" *Greenliving.nationalgeographic.com*. National Geographic Society, n.d. (©1996-2013). Web. 10 Jan. 2013.

Brown, Dee. *Bury My Heart at Wounded Knee*. New York: Washington Square Press/Pocketbooks: 1981. Print.

Burger King – Have It Your Way. Bk.com. Burger King Corporation, 2011. Web. 16 June 2011.

"California Admission Day September 9, 1850." *Www.parks.ca.gov*. State of California, 2013. Web. 10 Jan. 2013.

"California Condor (Gymnogyps Californianus)." *Npca.org*. National Parks Conservation Association, 2011. Web. 13 June 2011.

Caron, Mona. "El Camino." *Monacaron.com*. n.d. Web. 9 June 2011..

"The Chumash People of California." *Sbnature.org*. The Santa Barbara Museum of History. 2011. Web. 7 June 2011.

"Church History: El Pueblo de Nuestra Señora la Reina de los Angeles de Porciúncula." *Catholic.org*. Catholic Online, 15 Aug. 2005. Web. 10 Feb. 2013.

Coxhead, Averil. "Academic Word List." *Victoria.ac.nz*. V. U. of Wellington, NZ. 28 Nov. 2011. Web. 7 Oct. 2013.

"Delores Del Rio." *Imdb.com*. Imdb.com, an Amazon.com company, n.d., (© 1190-2013). Web. 14 Jan. 2013.

DeLyser, Dydia. *Ramona Memories*. Minneapolis: University of Minnesota Press, 2005. Print.

Didier, Suzanna. "Water Bottle Pollution Facts." *Greenliving.nationalgeographic.com*. National Geographic Society n.d. (©1996-2013). Web. 10 Jan. 2013.

"Discover the Oldest House in Los Angeles: Avila Adobe." *Elpueblo.lacity.org*. City of Los Angeles, 2011. Web. 14 Jan. 2013.

Dunitz, Robin J. *Street Gallery: Guide to 1000 Los Angeles Murals*. Los Angeles: RJD Enterprises, 1993. Print.

"Early El Pueblo History." *Elpueblo.lacity.org*. City of Los Angeles, 2011. Web. 14 Jan. 2013.

"El Camino Real (California)." *Wikipedia.org*. Wikimedia Foundation, 16 May 2011. Web. 9 June 2011.

"Facts at a Glance." *Cntower.ca*. Canada Lands Company, n.d. Web. 10 Jan. 2013.

Faigin, Daniel P. "Trails and Roads: El Camino Real." *Cahighways.org*. 9 June 2011. Web. 9 June 2011.

"Farmers Market: A Rich History." *Farmersmarketla.com*. A. F. Gilmore Company, 2006-2010. Web. 28 June 2011.

Four Directions Institute. "Gabrielino." *Fourdir.com*. Four Directions Press, 13 July 2007. Web. 7 June 2011.

"Full Throttle: The World's Tallest and Fastest Looping Roller Coaster." *Www.sixflags.com*. Six Flags, n.d. (© 2013). Web. 25 Mar. 2013.

Fumagalli, Barbara. Personal Interview on art media. 3 Jan 2013.

Gerstler, Amy. "Depot of Dreams." *Westways* March/April 2001: 16-17. Print.

The Getty. Getty.edu. The J. Paul Getty Trust, n.d. Web. 15 June 2011.

Glenday, Craig, Ed. "Michael Jackson Dies at 50." *Guinnessworldrecords.com*. Guinness World Records, 26 Jun 2009. Web. 27 May 2011.

"Griffith Observatory." *GriffithObservatory.org*. The City of Los Angeles Department of Recreation and Parks, n.d. Web. 14 June 2011.

"Griffith Park: General Information." *Laparks.org*. City of Los Angeles Department of Recreation and Parks, n.d., Web. 14 June 2011.

Grody, Steve. *Graffiti L. A.: Street Styles and Art*. New York: Abrams, 2006. Print.

"History of Native American Gaming." *Santainezchumash.org*. Santa Inez Band of Chumash Indians, 2009. Web. 10 Oct. 2012.

History of the Getty Villa. Video Dir. Peter Kirby courtesy of the J.P. Getty Trust. 2006. *Getty.edu*. Web. 15 June 2011.

Hooker, Richard. "The Iroquois League." *Public.wsu.edu*. Washington State Univ., 6 June 1999. Web. 8 June 2011.

"How to Understand and Use the Nutrition Facts Label." *Fda.gov*. U.S Department of Health and Human Services, 11 2004. Web. 22 June 2011.

"The Invention of Levi's® 501® Jeans." *Levistrauss.com*. Levi Strauss & Co., 2010. Web. 15 June 2011.

Jackson, Helen Hunt. *Ramona*. New York: Signet Classic- Penguin, 2002. Print.

Jacobs, Jason. "LA Zoo Lion Passes Away." *Lazoo.org*. The Greater Los Angeles Zoo Association. n.d. Web. 12 June 2011.

"Janet Jackson Biography." *Biography.com*. A & E Television Networks, 2011. Web. 27 May 2011.

Jorgensen, Lawrence C. "Making History: A Chronicle of the Valley's Past." *San-fernando.ca.us*. The City of San Fernando, n.d. Web. 9 June 2011.

Kashner, Sam. "Elizabeth Taylor's Closing Act." *Vanity Fair* June 2011: 146-152, 201-204. Print.
Kielbasa, John R. "Miguel Leonis Adobe." *Laokay.com.* The Okay Network, 1997. Web. 10 June 2011.
"Lactose Intolerance." *Digestive.niddk.nih.gov.* National Institute of Diabetes and Digestive and Kidney Diseases, June 2009. Web.16 June 2011.
"LA's Original Peoples." *Laalmanac.com.* Given Place Media, 1998-2011. Web. 7 June 2011.
"Life of Pío Pico Last Mexican Governor of California." *Piopico.org.* Friends of Pío Pico, 2004. Web. 14 Jan. 2013.
"List of Awards and Nominations Received by Janet Jackson." *Wikipedia.org.* Wikimedia Foundation, Inc., 23 May 2011. Web. 27 May 2011.
"List of English Irregular Verbs." *Wikipedia.org.* Wikimedia Foundation, Inc., 29 Mar. 2011. Web. 28 May 2011.
Lord, Rosemary. *Los Angeles Then & Now.* San Diego: Thunder Bay Press, 2002. Print.
Mapquest.org. Mapquest, Inc., 2011. Web. 30 May 2011.
McCall, Lynne, et al. *California's Chumash Indians.* Santa Barbara: EZ Nature Books, 2002. Print.
McCawley, William. *The First Angelinos: The Gabrielino Indians of Los Angeles.* Banning: Malki Museum Press/Ballena Press Cooperative, 1996. Print.
McDonald's – I'm Lovin' It. Mcdonalds.com. McDonald's, 2010-2011. Web. 16 June 2011.
"Michael Jackson Bio." *Michaeljackson.com.* Sony Music Entertainment, 2011. Web. 27 May 2011.
"Michael Jackson Biography." *Biography.com.* A & E Television Networks, 2011. Web. 27 May 2011.
"Musso and Frank Grill." *Www.mussoandfrankgrill.com.* N.p., n.d. Web. 20 Oct. 2012.
Nall, Rachell. "Statistics on Pollution." *Greenliving.nationalgeographic.com.* National Geographic Society n.d. (©1996-2013). Web. 10 Jan. 2013.
"Native American Wisdom." *FirstPeople.us.* First People of America and First People of Canada: Turtle Island, 13 Apr 2011. Web. 23 May 2011.
Neihardt, John G. *Black Elk Speaks.* 1932. *Firstpeople.us: Native American Articles.* n.d.. Web. 23 May 2011.
"The Nethercutt Collection." *Nethercuttcollection.org.* The Nethercutt Collection, 2008. Web. 15 June 2011.
"Nutrition Information." *Chilis.com.* Brinker International, 2009. Web. 22 June 2011.
The Official Website for Gene Autry. Autry.com. Gene Autry Entertainment, 2011. Web. 11 June 2011.
"Once Upon a Time . . ." *Brinker.com.* Brinker International, 2009. Web. 22 June 2011.
"Orcutt Ranch Horticultural Center Rancho Sombra Del Roble." *Laparks.org.* City of Los Angeles Department of Recreation and Parks, 2011. Web. 11 June 2011.
Patterson, Frank. "Fajita." *Cookeryonline.com.* Cookery Online, 14 Oct 2003. Web. 22 June 2011.
Peterson, Chris W. "Return to the Ice Age: La Brea Exploration Guide." *Tarpits.org.* Natural History Museum of Los Angeles County. 2002. Web. 31 May 2011.
"Plastic Pollution." *Takepart.com.* Participant Media, n.d. (© 2008-2013). Web. 10 Jan. 2013.
"Plastics." *Www.epa.gov.* U. S. Environmental Protection Agency, 19 Nov. 2012. Web. 10 Jan. 2013.
"The Red Cars of Los Angeles." *Usc.edu.* The University of Southern California, 15 Jan. 2002. Web. 28 June 2011.
Redish, Laura and Orrin Lewis. "Haudenosaunee (Iroquois) Indian Fact Sheet." *Bigorrin.org.* Native Languages of the Americas, 1998-2011. Web. 8 June 2011.
Salas, Abel. "Another Jewel for the Mural Capital of the World." *Los Angeles Times,* 15 Sept. 2002. Web. 14 Jan. 2013.
"San Fernando Rey de España." *Missionscalifornia.com.* Pentacle Press, 2003-2011. Web. 9 June 2011.
Schaefer, Athanasius. "San Fernando Rey de España." *Athanasius.com.* N.p., n.d. Web. 9 June 2011.
Scharf, Walter, and Don Black. "Ben." Jobete Music Company, Inc., 1972. *Elyrics.net.* Web. 12 Feb. 2012.
Shaftel, George. "California." *World Book Encyclopedia,* 1961 ed. Print.
Simondi, Tom. "Nuestra Señora la Reina de Los Angeles." *Missiontour.org.* MissionTour, 2006-2011. Web. 10 Feb. 2013.
"Starbucks." *Wikipedia.org.* Wikimedia Foundation, 22 June 2011. Web. 22 June 2011.
"Starbucks Secret Menu." *Starbuckssecretmenu.net.* Starbucks Secret Menu, 2012. Web. 10 Oct. 2012.
"Starbucks Secret Menu Items." *Www.ranker.com.* N.d. (© 2013 Ranker). Web. 30 Mar. 2013.
Timbrook, Jan. *Chumash Ethnobotany.* Berkeley: Heyday Books, 2007. Print.
"Vegetables and Fruits: Get Plenty Every Day." *Hsph.harvard.edu.* Harvard School of Public Health, 2013. Web. 10 Jan. 2013.
Vetter, Rick. "Myth of the Brown Recluse: Fact, Fear, and Loathing." *Spiders.ucr.edu.* University of California, Riverside., 16 Nov. 2011. Web. 10 Jan. 2012.
Wallach, Ruth. "Los Angeles Murals." *Public Art in Los Angeles. Publicartinla.com.* USC Libraries, Apr. 2010. Web 14 Jan. 2013.
Weatherford, Jack. *Indian Givers: How the Indians of the Americas Transformed the World.* New York: Crown Publishers, 1988. Print.
Williams, Kam. "Conversations with Janet Jackson." *Filmgordon.wordpress.com.* Word Press, 26 Oct 2010. Web. 27 May 2011.
"Wishtoyo Foundation's Chumash Discovery Village." *Wishtoyo.org.* Wishtoyo Foundation, 31 May 2011. Web. 7 June 2011.
"Zoo History." *Lazoo.org.* The Greater Los Angeles Zoo Association. n.d. Web. 12 June 2011.

Made in the USA
San Bernardino, CA
20 May 2014